Best Sights to See at

Rocky Mountain National Park

By Rob Bignell

Atiswinic Press · Ojai, Calif.

BEST SIGHTS TO SEE AT ROCKY MOUNTAIN NATIONAL PARK

A GUIDEBOOK IN THE BEST SIGHTS TO SEE SERIES

Copyright Rob Bignell, 2018

Atiswinic Press
Ojai, Calif. 93023
dayhikingtrails.wordpress.com

ISBN 978-1-948872-00-3

Cover design by Rob Bignell
Cover photo of Bear Lake at Rocky Mountain National Park

Manufactured in the United States of America
First printing April 2018

For Kieran

Contents

Introduction

I magine a place where magnificent peaks soar more than two-and-a-half miles high, where alpine lakes reflect snow-capped mountains and evergreens in crystal clear water, where blooming wildflowers fill meadows with color while towering forests shade sun-dappled paths, where rushing creeks and waterfalls are as common as driveways in a suburb. The place is real: it's called Rocky Mountain National Park.

Established more than a century ago, Rocky Mountain National Park is one of the nation's most popular with 4.5 million visitors a year. While most come to see the majestic Colorado mountains, they are surprised by the sighting of bald eagles wheeling overhead or the thrilling bugle of a bull elk in the distance. Others discover the glory of the rising sun across the rocky tundra or delight in frolicking across a snow field in July. And at night when darkness veils the mountains, they gasp as the Milky Way shines more brilliantly than they've ever seen.

But with the park's incredible size of 415 square miles and the large crowds, how can *you* ensure that you'll see its main sights when vacationing or driving through? That's what "Best Sights to See at Rocky Mountain National Park" answers. In this volume, we've listed the top 10 most popular sights and detailed day hiking trails to best experience them, as well as offered similar hikes in the park.

Geology

About a billion years ago, molten lava formed large amounts

of granite in what is now Colorado. Then, roughly 500 million years ago, the land began to sink and fill with sediment, forming several rock strata.

Some 300 million years ago, the land rebounded, and a range known as the Ancestral Rocky Mountains formed. It eroded over a period of 150 million years, covering its stubs in its own sediment. A series of erosion and sandstone/shale formations occurred over the next 220 million years.

The Front Range of the park formed about 80 million years ago during the Laramide Orogeny. (An *orogeny* is a mountain-building event.) At that time, two tectonic plates – the Kula and the Farallon – collided with North America's western coast. As those plates slid under North America, rock set down over the previous billion years bunched up and wrinkled; those "wrinkles" are the mountains we now see.

Immediately after being thrust upward, the park and the rest of the Rockies looked much different than today, though, as it was a plateau more than 19,000 feet high. Then about 60 million years ago, this plateau began to erode, forming valleys and summits. The peaks today mostly top out in the 14,000-feet range, about a mile lower than the plateau. Hikers at the national park can see one of the Front Range's most prominent 14ers, Longs Peak, via the **Bluebird Lake Trail**.

Periods of glaciation that started about 1.8 million years ago deeply shaped the park and Rockies into the landscape we know today. U-shaped valleys as well as cirques (concave-shaped valleys) are signs of past glaciers in the area. The last ice age ended around 11,000 years ago, though remnants of some glaciers still remain. One easy and scenic route to see how glaciers shaped the park is the **Alberta Falls Trail**, where a waterfall tumbles over a creek that runs from a gorge created by a glacier. You can enter that gorge via the **Mills Lake Trail**.

Geography

Rocky Mountain National Park marks only a small portion of Colorado's Front Range. Indeed, those advocating establishment of the national park during the early 20th century sought to protect a million acres but got a park only a quarter that size. Still, the park is quite representative of the Southern Rocky Mountains, which stretch from just northwest of Cheyenne south to Santa Fe and at its widest from the Great Plains to the desert along the Colorado-Utah border.

The park's terrain is entirely mountainous and at a high altitude – the lowest point is at 7,860 feet, nearly a mile-and-a-half above sea level. The highest point is **Longs Peak** at 14,259 feet, and more than 77 mountains soar higher than 12,000 feet.

Because of this, the park's geography perhaps is best thought of vertically and in 3D rather than horizontally across a 2D map. Elevation is the main determinant of how different parts of the park appear.

Indeed, three distinct ecosystems make up the park. The lowest and most visited is the montane ecosystem, which ranges from 5,600 to 9,500 feet. There you can find mountain meadows and green forests of ponderosa pine, Douglas-fir, and lodgepole pine. A great hike through the montane ecosystem is the **Alberta Falls Trail**.

Above it is the subalpine ecosystem, which begins between 9,000-9,500 feet and continues to about 11,000 feet. With higher snowfalls, the winters are longer and colder than at the montane elevations below. Trees here include the hardier limber pine, Engelmann spruce, and subalpine fir. The park's **Bear Lake Loop** explores the subalpine region.

The highest ecosystem is the alpine tundra, which begins at 11,000 feet. It's mostly treeless with only the most robust of plants able to grow there. A good day hike cutting through this low-oxygen terrain is the **Alpine Ridge Trail**.

Through these ecosystems run 473 miles of streams, many feeding the park's 147 lakes. The park is the headwaters for several important rivers in Colorado, including the Big Thompson, Cache la Poudre and Fall, and for the most important waterway in the Southwest, the **Colorado**.

The diversity of landscapes across the park serves as the home for more than a thousand kinds of flowering plants, 280 bird species, 141 types of butterflies, and 66 mammals. At the park's high elevation, though, only one kind of snake – the harmless garter – can survive. Most flora and wildlife here can be found well beyond the park boundaries.

History

The earliest indication of people being in what is now Rocky Mountain National Park dates to 10,000 years ago when mammoth hunters lost projectile points on Trail Ridge. Use of the mountains as a thoroughfare for hunters continued for millennia.

Indeed, during the 1800s, the Ute and Arapaho hunted and traveled across the park, but there's no sign of permanent settlements. The Ute primarily resided west of the Continental Divide near Grand Lake and came onto the prairie to hunt bison. The Arapaho lived east of the divide on the Plains and hunted the area that is now Estes Park. Pawnee, Sioux and Apache also crossed this region.

Major Stephen Long first explored the region for the United States in 1820. His expedition didn't enter the mountains, but he recorded sighting the park's highest point – Longs Peak – which was named for him.

European-Americans began settling the area in 1843 when hunter Rufus Sage set up his home there. In 1858, Joel Estes sought elk in the area to feed Colorado miners. After the elk were wiped out and cattle grazing in the high mountain meadows proved unprofitable, Estes and his neighbors decided to offer boarding to those wanting to see the Front Range's spectacular sites. Thus began the region's tourism industry.

News about exploration of the area helped fuel tourism. Explorer John Wesley Powell made the first recorded ascent of Longs Peak in 1868. Local homesteader Abner Sprague peakbagged a number of other area mountains in the years that followed.

Teenage miner Enos Mills' building of a cabin in Tahosa Valley during 1884 certainly didn't attract much attention but it proved to be a pivotal moment in the park's history. A few years later, Mills spent time in California with American naturalist John Muir and afterward returned to Longs Peak, where he dedicated his life to conservation. Mills since has become known as the "Father of Rocky Mountain National Park."

Freelan Stanley, inventor of photographic plates, moved to the area in 1905, opened an inn, and became a leader in the tourism economy. He worked to return elk to the park by transplanting the species from Montana.

The combined efforts of these men and many others ultimately led to the creation and opening of Rocky Mountain National Park in 1915.

That same decade, Fall River Road was constructed to link Estes Park and Grand Lake in the summer, increasing accessibility to the Front Range's interior. Then in the Great Depression, the better quality Trail Ridge Road was constructed, allowing motorists to discover the park in the postwar boom.

In September 2013, a flood damaged a number of the park's east-side trails and bridges when 18 inches of rain fell over three days. Communities at lower elevations suffered far more damage than did the park, but even today short detours remain on some trails to avoid fallen trees, lost water crossings, and unstable slopes.

Park Layout

Rocky Mountain National Park is a roughly square-shaped wilderness surrounded by the Roosevelt National Forest on the east and north sides and the Arapaho National Forest on the south and west.

Most of the national park's best sites rest along or near U.S. Hwy. 34, which enters the park in two locations: the most popular one on the northeast side a few miles west of Estes Park and leading to the Fall River Visitor Center; and then the southwest corner at Grand Lake. Also known as Trail Ridge Road, the highway offers access to and parallels the famous Old Fall River Road, the precursor to the federal highway, the Alpine Visitor Center, the Continental Divide, the Colorado River, and the Kawuneeche Valley with its visitor center.

U.S. Hwy. 36 also offers access to a couple of regions south of the Hwy. 34 entrance. Among them are the Moraine Park, Bear Lake, Glacier Gorge, and Loch Vale areas. The Beaver Meadows and the Moraine Park visitor centers can be accessed via this highway.

A few other interesting sites along the park's eastern border can be reached via Colo. Hwy. 7, which runs from Estes Park to Meeker Park and Allenspark. Among them are Tahosa Valley – which includes famous Longs Peak, the park's highest point at 14,259 feet – and the Wild Basin.

Continuing west on Hwy. 34 brings visitors deeper into the Rocky Mountains and to the Continental Divide at Milner Pass, some 10,758 feet high. The divide cuts roughly diagonally

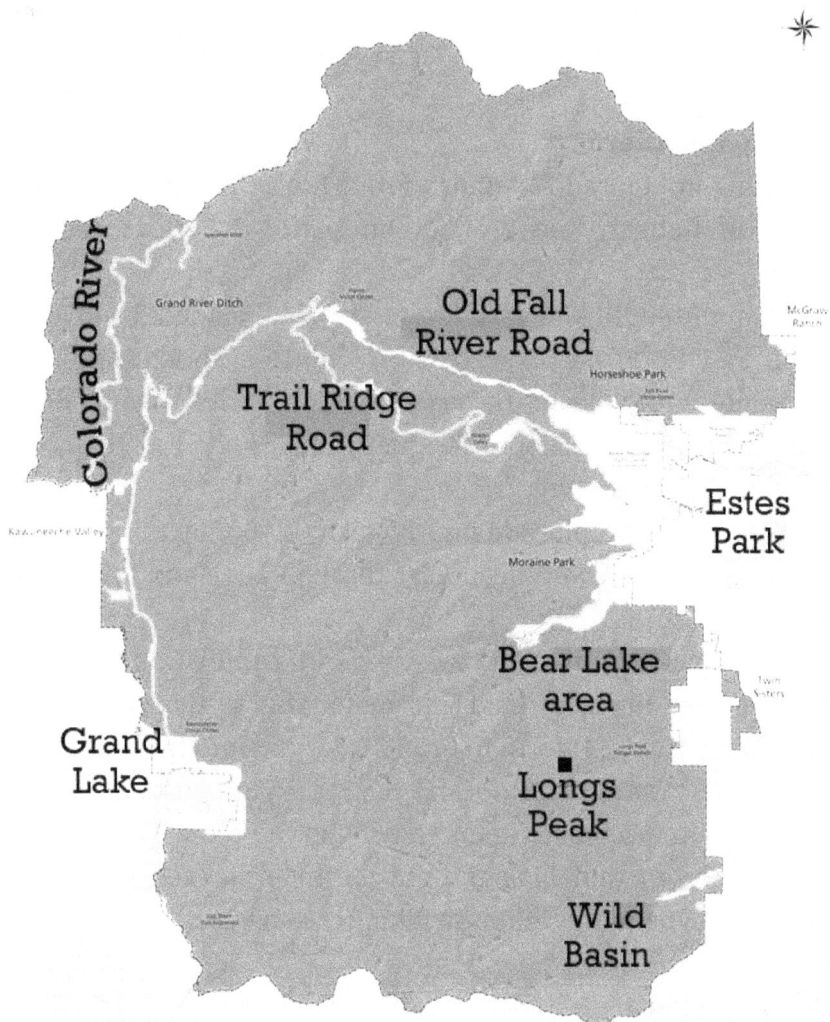

Rocky Mountain National Park, courtesy of Colorado DOT.

through the park. All water east of the divide ultimately ends up in the Atlantic while water west of it flows into the Pacific. The Alpine Visitor Center is located at this high elevation.

After crossing Milner Pass, Hwy. 34 runs mainly south to the Grand Lake area. The Kawuneeche Valley, from which the Colorado River flows, can be found here, as well as Shadow Mountain Lake and Lake Granby. There the road exits the park and joins U.S. Hwy. 40, which connects with Interstate 70.

How to Get There

Sitting in Colorado's famous Front Range about 90 minutes north of Denver, Rocky Mountain National Park is easy to reach.

From the south and east, Interstates 76, 70 and 25 converge upon Denver. From there, take I-25 north then exit onto U.S. Hwy. 36, which heads through Boulder on its way to Estes Park. You then can choose to enter the park via U.S. Hwys. 34 or 36 or Colorado Hwy. 7.

If coming into Colorado on I-25 from Wyoming to the north, exit onto Hwy 34 and head east through Loveland into Estes Park.

Those arriving from the west via I-70 can exit on U.S. Hwy 40 and head north through the mountains to Grandby. From there, take Hwy. 34 north to Grand Lake and into the park.

Anyone visiting who doesn't live at a high altitude should take a day to acclimate upon arriving in the park. There really is less oxygen that high up, and altitude sickness can be a problem if you jump right into hiking the sights.

When to Visit

June through October marks the best time to visit Rocky Mountain National Park.

Summer temperatures typically top out in the 80s with lows hitting the 40s at night. Remember, though, that each 1000-foot gain on average means a 3 degree drop in temperature, so you may want to carry extra clothing depending on your destination. For example, if the high in Estes Park is 70 degrees, expect it to be a crisp 57 at the Alpine Visitor Center.

During spring and summer, sun-drenched skies are common during the morning, but afternoon thunderstorms can form quickly and result in lightning, hail and high winds. If clouds build up anytime between 9 a.m.-noon, you probably have about two hours before a storm; you're usually safe if clouds build after noon. If clouds build before 9 a.m., the day probably will be lost to rain.

Beware that July is the busiest month, and with the national park's growing popularity, certain sections – especially those closest to Estes Park and attractions right off the road – can be crowded.

Post-Labor Day September often marks an ideal time to visit. Not only are there smaller crowds, but dry weather and cooler temperatures (though often only reaching the 50s for a high) dominate. There's the added bonus of changing leaf colors at the lower elevations and bugling bull elks in the distance. By mid-October, though, snow usually falls, closing Trail Ridge Road through winter until late May.

Kids Activities

A trip to Rocky Mountain National Park can be an educational experience for kids – though they may be having too much fun to even notice that they're learning!

The park delivers a variety of great activities that children can participate in from spring through autumn. Among the many offerings:

• **Ranger-led events** – Free programs for kids throughout the park focus on a range of interests, from wildlife and plants found in the Rocky Mountains to preserving local natural and cultural treasures. Check the current park newspaper for topics, times and locations.

• **Junior Ranger Kids** – Kids between the ages of 5-12 can become a Junior Ranger. They'll first need to obtain a Junior Ranger booklet (available online and at any park visitor center) and complete its activities, and then they can receive a Junior Ranger badge.

• **Junior Ranger Headquarters** – From late June to mid-August, several ranger-led programs for kids are held at Hidden Valley off of Trail Ridge Road. Programs are offered four times a day, every day of the week, with each lasting about a half-hour.

Maps

To properly prepare for any hike, you should examine maps before hitting the trail and bring them with you (See the bonus Day Hiking Primer for more.). No guidebook can reproduce a map as well as the aerial photographs or topographical maps that you can find online for free. To that end, a companion website to this book offers printable maps for each featured trail at *dayhiking trails.wordpress.com/trail-maps.*

Best Sights

Rocky Mountains National Park is so large that unless you spend years there, you won't see all it offers. So when you've only a few days at best to visit the park, what are the absolute must-see sights? Following are the park's 10 best spots and the day hiking trails for getting to them.

Longs Peak is Rocky Mountain National Park's highest point.

14,000-Foot Peaks

Bluebird Lake Trail

At 14,259 feet, Longs Peak is one of Colorado's most visibly prominent Fourteeners – a mountain more than 14,000 feet high – on the Front Range. Among the best views of it can be had on the Bluebird Lake Trail in the park's Wild Basin area.

The trail is not for the timid or physically unfit. This 12.6-miles round trip includes an elevation gain of 2,478 feet.

Your effort will be worth it, though. Along the hike, you'll pass four waterfalls, a cascades, an alpine lake, and be treated to spectacular scenery.

The trail sits in the park's southeast corner. To reach the trailhead, from Allenspark village, take Colo. Hwy. 7 north. Turn left/west onto County Road 84, following it north to the Wild Basin Lodge. Go left/northwest onto County Road 115 (note that the last stretch is a narrow, gravel road), parking in the lot of the Wild Basin Summer Trailhead.

Take the trail southwest into the pine forest. You're at 8500 feet, which already is extremely high, so stay alert for altitude sickness.

At 0.3 miles from the trailhead, you can take a short spur to Lower Copeland Falls on North Saint Vrain Creek. It's only about 5-feet high but a pleasant spot to take a break. About 0.1 miles later is Upper Copeland Falls.

Next the trail crosses Sandbeach Creek and parallels North Saint Vrain Creek.

At 1.4 miles from the trailhead is Pine Ridge Campground. There the trail splits; go left/southwest. The trail crosses the creek once (If you pass the Tahosa Campground, you've taken the wrong trail.).

You'll arrive at an unnamed cascades/waterfall with a 15-foot drop in 0.2 miles. Sometimes this is confused with Calypso

Cascades. That's coming up, though.

About 2.2 miles from the trailhead, you'll reach the next trail junction. Go right/west. In short order, you'll cross Cony Creek.

The 100-foot Calypso Cascades are downstream. The best time to see them is early summer, as by September waterflow can be a bit sparse. At the cascades, you'll also get excellent views of Longs Peak – the highest in the national park – and Mount Meeker, both of which are to the north. The two peaks are referred to as the Twin Guides. Longs Peak is the northernmost of Colorado's famed Fourteeners.

Next the trail meanders to the northwest, gaining about 300 feet elevation until at the 2.7 mile mark from the trailhead it crosses Ouzel Creek via a log footbridge. Forty-foot high Ouzel Falls is upstream and visible from the log. For a closer look, you also can take a spur to the falls, which is at 9370 feet elevation. The spur adds about 0.5 miles to the hike.

At 3 miles from the trailhead, the route divides. Bluebird Lake Trail goes left/southwest while Thunder Lake Trail goes right/northwest. The National Park Service constructed the pair in 1926.

Take the Bluebird Lake Trail into Wild Basin. Along the way, you'll pass the Aspen Knoll Campground. Ouzel Creek is to the left/south.

About 3.5 miles from the trailhead, you'll walk through a forest of burned out tree trunks. In 1978, the Ouzel Fire, caused by lightning, burned more than a thousand acres here. The blaze took nearly four months to put out.

A spur on the left leads to Ouzel Lake at the 4.6-miles mark. Taking it adds a mile round tip to the hike.

Continue straight/southwest on the Bluebird Lake Trail. The route now becomes rugged and steep with a fair amount of talus. Wildflowers abound in spring and summer, though.

Ouzel Falls

Next you'll cross Upper Ouzel Creek, which the trail hugs until arriving at Bluebird Lake, where it ends at the 6.3-miles mark. Three peaks surround the boulder-ringed lake – 13,176-foot Mt. Copeland to the south, 12,716-foot Ouzel Peak to the west, and 12,632-foot Mahana Peak to the northwest. The lake is at 10,978 feet elevation.

At one time, Bluebird Lake was dammed with a 58-foot high and 200-foot long wall. In 1989-90, the park service removed more than 5 million pounds of concrete and rebar from the dam – all via helicopter!

Whenever at this elevation, always keep a watch for fast-changing mountain weather. In addition, pack as if you are going stay the night, just in case weather makes heading back impossible.

Longs Peak summit

While certainly no day hike, you also can walk to the summit of Longs Peak. Around 15,000 mountaineers try it each year.

To reach that trailhead, from Allenspark drive north on County Road 7. Turn left/west onto Longs Peak Road. Upon entering the park and just before the campground curve left/south. The trailhead is past the ranger station at the end of the road. The East Longs Peaks Trail runs 13.6 miles one-way. You start at an elevation of 9418 feet and will gain 4786 feet. It's a well-marked trail.

The trail initially parallels Alpine Brook then later crosses it as well as Larkspur Creek and Boulder Brook. A spur leads to Chasm Lake. Ultimately, the trail ends just past an area known as Boulderfield, where there is a campground.

Due to the high altitude, you definitely need to be physically fit and spend a couple of weeks acclimating your body before attempting this adventure.

Waterfalls

Alberta Falls Trail

Lush green woodland, a waterfall, and a Rocky Mountain high await day hikers on the Alberta Falls Trail near Estes Park. The 1.4-mile out-and-back trail sits in the heart of Rocky Mountain National Park. Seventy-two of the mountain peaks in the national park rise 12,000 feet above sea level.

Because of the high altitudes, summer marks the best time to hike the trail. However, because of the trail's ease and its big payoff – the waterfall – expect it be somewhat crowded.

To reach the trailhead, from Estes Park travel east on U.S. Hwy. 36, turning left/south onto Bear Lake Road. You'll drive through some fantastic scenery for about eight miles to the Glacier Gorge Trailhead parking lot, which is near the road's terminus. The trailhead sits at the lot's southwest corner.

With a trailhead elevation of 9240 feet, be aware that there's less oxygen up there, so pace yourself. In addition, you'll go uphill on the way to the waterfalls for a 200-foot gain.

The dirt path through evergreens connects with the Glacier Gorge Trail in about 650 feet. Go left/south and in less than 50 feet turn onto the trail to your right/southeast.

To the northwest is Hallett Peak and the Continental Divide. The peak rises to 12,270 feet with pretty Bear Lake sitting below it.

The trail crosses Tyndall Creek then splits. Go left/southeast. You'll know you've gone the wrong way if you cross Tyndall Creek again.

The forest here is mixed pines with aspen groves. You can almost hear John Denver singing in the distance. At the very least, if you've never visited the Rockies before, you'll get a good understanding on the trail of what he meant by "Now he

Alberta Falls tumbles over a 30-foot drop.

walks in quiet solitude, the forest and the streams/Seeking grace in every step he takes."

About 800 feet from the last trail junction, you'll cross Chaos Creek. The trail meanders a bit then veers south as paralleling Glacier Creek to your left. If hiking during early autumn, the changing aspen leaf colors makes for great scenery.

Alberta Falls appears within 1200 feet. It thunders over a small gorge with a 30-foot drop. It is named for Alberta Sprague, the wife of one of Este Park's first white settlers. Her husband, Abner Sprague, became the first person to pay an entrance fee into Rocky Mountain National Park in 1939.

Alberta Falls is a great place for a picnic if you'd like to carry lunch in your backpack. There's a good chance that you'll share the area with painters capturing the falls on canvas.

While the trail does continue onward, the falls marks a good spot to turn around.

Other Rocky Mountain Waterfalls

Rocky Mountain National Park is a waterfall lovers' paradise. With 31 named waterfalls and many more unnamed and seasonal falls in the backcountry, they can't all be seen in one visit. Among the park's best falls and the trails to see them are:

• **Adams Falls** – Rainbows shine through the 55-foot-high falls' mist during the early morning hours. Adams Falls sits at the end of a 0.6 miles round trip in-and-out trail. Use the East Inlet Trailhead near Grand Lake.

• **Bridal Veil Falls** – A 6.4-miles round trip hike heads past historic McGraw Ranch and through an aspen forest to the 40-foot falls. Start at the Cow Creek Trailhead.

• **Cascade Falls** – The wide waterfall offers flat rocks perfect for picnicking. The 3.5-mile hike through lodgepole pines starts at the North Inlet Trailhead near Grand Lake.

- **Chasm Falls** – A mere 100 feet from Old Fall River Road, this is perhaps the most accessible waterfall in the park. There the Fall River cuts through a narrow gorge and drops 30 feet.
- **Columbine Falls** – The 110-foot waterfall is about 6-miles round trip from the Longs Peak trailhead. After Roaring Fork tumbles over the cliffside, it gathers in Peacock Pool.
- **Copeland Falls** – Two small waterfalls – an upper and lower that drop a combined 12 feet – are a short distance apart on the first waterfall from the Wild Basin Trailhead, a mere 0.8 miles round trip. Another 1.4 miles up the trail is the Calypso Cascades, which tumbles 90 feet over boulders.
- **Fern Falls** – The 60-foot waterfall casts a fine mist across the forested trail. Seeing the falls requires a 5.4-miles round trip hike on the way to Fern Lake.
- **Horseshoe Falls** – A long cascade waterfall, Horseshoe Falls can be seen from the Alluvial Fan Trail in a short 0.4-miles round trip hike. In total, water drops 250 feet here.
- **MacGregor Falls** – The waterfall tumbles 22 feet on Black Canyon Creek. Park at the Lumpy Ridge Trailhead lot and head west on Lumpy Ridge Trail for a 6.2-mile round trip.
- **Ouzel Falls** – The waterfall drops 40 feet over a cliffside and across boulders. It's a 5.4-mile round trip hike from the Wild Basin Trailhead; hiking to this trail allows you to also see Copeland Falls and the Calypso Cascades.
- **Timberline Falls** – Though a long day hike at 8-miles round trip, the effort is worth it, as the falls drops 100 feet with a great view of The Loch and the mountain valley. Use the Glacier Gorge trailhead.
- **West Creek Falls** – This is a great waterfall for those looking to get away from crowds. A spur off the North Boundary Trail, you'll walk 4.75 miles round trip from the Cow Creek Trailhead to the 22-foot falls.

Mountain Wildlife

Lawn Lake Trail

Day hikers stand a good chance of spotting a variety of montane wildlife on the Lawn Lake Trail.

The 12.5-miles round trip from Fall River to Lawn Lake is just a segment of the overall trail. Be forewarned, though: Because of its high altitude, the elevation gain (2447 feet), a rocky trail surface, and the length, this is not a hike for the unfit.

In addition, the trail usually is only open May through October, as heavy snowfall at the high elevation closes the road in winter.

To reach the trailhead, from Estes Park, take U.S. Hwy. 34 (aka Fall River Road) east into the park. Once past the Sheep Lakes Information Station but before Fall River, turn right/northwest onto Old Fall River Road. A parking lot is on the right/northwest.

Follow the access trail northeast and in a couple of hundred feet, pick up the Lawn Lake Trail. Go left/northwest on the trail. The elevation is about 8540 feet above sea level.

The trail heads through lodgepole, fir and aspen forest covering a wide, flat basin in the Mummy Range. As the trail heads toward the treeline, it offers habitat for a variety of animals.

Mule deer are quite common at this elevation. Up to three feet tall at the shoulder, they can weigh anywhere from a hundred to 300 pounds. Usually by midsummer, mothers bring out their fawns.

The deer have extremely large ears that resemble those of a mule. They tend to live in the park's lower hills and in light forests. About 500 of them gather in Estes Valley each winter.

At 0.55 miles, the trail begins its steady climb up over Horseshoe Park. North American elk are common here in autumn. The large males can stand up to 5 feet at the shoulder

Bull elk at Rocky Mountain National Park

weigh several hundred pounds. Their new young usually can be spotted in early to midsummer.

Bull elks make a distinctive bugling sound each autumn to mark the beginning of the breeding season. Typically they can be seen in Moraine Park grazing during summer and the lower meadows during fall. About 300-400 elk winter in the park and another 500-600 winter in Estes Park.

During winter, bighorn sheep sometimes come down to this elevation for salt licks. The muscular males are no taller than mule deer at the shoulder and usually top out at 300 pounds. The females are about half that size.

The bighorn ram has served as the park's on and off official symbol, most recently appearing on its centennial logo. Bighorn often can be spotted at Big Thompson Canyon and Sheep-Horseshoe Park between 9 a.m. and 3 p.m.

At a mile from the trailhead, the route comes to the east bank of Roaring River, which is full of riffles. Much of the river valley here formed during the summer 1982 flashflood. Though scars remain, vegetation during the intervening decades has reclaimed most of the lost ground. Among those trees is aspen, which turn a beautiful gold each autumn along the river banks.

The junction for Ypsilon Lake Trail is at 1.4 miles. Continue right/north alongside the river.

In late summer, berries and mushrooms growing along the river attract black bears. With adults about 5-6 feet long, they can weigh up to 600 pounds. Though appearing fat, they're quite muscular and can outrun a human being.

At 2 miles, the trail runs on a level bank of the river, allowing for quick travel. Bighorn Mountain (summit at 11,463 feet elevation) is to the right/east while Ypsilon Mountain (13,520 feet) rises to the northwest along the river's west bank.

While some hikers have reported wolves and foxes in this area, they more than likely saw coyotes, which at a distance easily can be confused their close relatives. About three to five feet long, they weigh up to 50 pounds and usually have gray-yellow-brown fur with bushy tails and a white underbelly. They are much smaller than wolves.

Coyotes have a well-earned reputation as survivors, they thrive in a park where concerted efforts at the beginning of the 20th century were made to remove them and wolves. The effort with wolves succeeded. Coyotes usually feed on rodents and deer but have been observed pack hunting bighorn lambs and ewes.

At 2.75 miles, the trail junctions a spur to a backcountry campsite. Upon reaching 3.5 miles, the trail begins a gradual rise in an increasingly diverse forest.

Another predator common in the national forest are cougars, though because of their solitary nature sightings are rare. If you see bark on a tree that is scratched off, a mountain lion probably was the culprit.

Males stretch up to eight feet long and weigh 200 pounds; they can jump 18 feet high and 40 feet long in a single bound. Rare to see, they are most frequently spotted on park's west side, especially near rocky canyons and meadows. An estimated 20-30 mountain lions live in the park.

At 4 miles from the trailhead, you've reach 10,000 feet. Mount Tileston's peak is to the right/east.

A number of small mammals also can be seen. Among the more unique ones is the yellow-bellied marmot. A member of the squirrel family, they grow up to two feet in length but weigh a mere 11 pounds. Usually they live in colonies of 10-20 individuals.

About 4.5 miles from the trailhead, the surrounding peaks begin to emerge. Fairchild Mountain (13,502 feet), Hagues Peak (13,560 feet) and Mummy Mountain (13,425 feet) ring this basin.

Other small animals living in the park and likely to be seen on the trail are chipmunks and snowshoe hares. One creature you won't see is the pika, which lives only above 11,000 feet.

At 5 miles, the transition to a spruce-fir forest begins. Then, about 5.65 miles from the trailhead is the intersection with Cow Creek Trail. Continue straight/left/north, briefly leaving Roaring River and paralleling a creek that flows into it. In short order, the trail rejoins Roaring River's east bank.

At 6 miles, the trail runs through a patchy forest of old growth spruce. This is the high point over Lawn Lake, which Roaring River flows out of.

You finally reach your destination – Lawn Lake – at 6.25

miles. Sitting at 10,987 feet elevation, it is the national park's largest subalpine lake. The lake was a reservoir until 1982 when the 26-foot earthen dam collapsed. An incredible 134,640 gallons of water roared down the river valley per *second*. The lake is now at its original level and popular with fishermen.

You can extend the hike by continuing around lake and into more rugged terrain. For a day hike, though, the trek to the lake is sufficient.

Notes: Watch weather reports; at high altitudes, thunderstorms can sneak up on you in summer. Horses, but not dogs, are allowed on the trail.

Other Trails to See Rocky Mountain Wildlife

A wide range of animals reside in Rocky Mountain National Park – but unlike bears or bison at Yosemite or Abert's squirrels at Grand Canyon – wildlife here is a bit more standoffish. That doesn't mean they can't be seen, just that you should be aware of where, when and how to spot them:

• **Moose** – The largest animal in the park, they can stand up to seven feet high at the shoulder and weigh 1500 pounds. With only 30-50 moose residing here, they are a rare sight. The best spot to see them is on the park's west side grazing along the Colorado River banks and in the Kawuneeche Valley.

• **Black bear** – Ranging 5-6 feet long and weighing between 200-600 pounds, black bears are an impressive sight. Despite their bulk, they easily can outrun a human being. The good news is that they are rarely seen, as they avoid people. Only about 20-24 black bears remain in the park with the few sightings occurring in the backcountry.

• **Pika** – Small mammals that look like hamsters, pikas actually are more closely related to rabbits. Weighing a mere six ounces, they sit on rock outcroppings and talus slopes near the treeline, especially around Rock Cut on the 0.6 miles round-trip Tundra Communities Trail off of Trail Ridge Road.

Montane Forests

Mills Lake Trail

Day hikers can explore a montane forest on the Mills Lake Trail.

Such forests cover much of this national park, which sits at high elevations. The trail runs 2.65 miles one-way (5.3 miles round trip) through a woods to a mountain lake at the base of Glacier Gorge.

To reach the trail, from Estes Park, head west on U.S. Hwy. 36. Turn onto Bear Lake Road, and drive eight miles to the Glacier Gorge Trailhead. A free park shuttle also runs there to the trailhead, and if starting later in the day, it's a good option to take as during peak tourist season, the parking lot fills quick.

The trailhead elevation is 9240 feet. Be aware that there's less oxygen that high up, and it thins even more as the trail gains 727 feet. Watch for signs of altitude sickness among yourself and your party.

Your hike begins by crossing Chaos Creek. At 0.25 miles from trailhead, the route joins Glacier Creek Trail. When the trails splits, go left to Mills Lake.

A montane forest consists of meandering rivers and creaks that run through open meadows surrounded by steep slopes. This makes for picturesque scenery, especially in summer when wildflowers blanket the meadows.

At 0.8 miles, the trail reaches its first highlight, Alberta Falls. The 30-foot waterfall on Glacier Creek sits at 9423 feet. From there, the trail climbs a hillside above Glacier Creek.

As walking through the meadows, you'll notice that different

Mills Lake

slopes tend to be dominated by specific kinds of trees. In fact, you can use these trees as a sort of compass.

South-facing slopes tend to be dry and so boast open stands of large ponderosa pines. Hiking through ponderosa pines always is a delight in summer, as bark, when warmed by the sun, is quite fragrant. In addition, you can tell the age of a ponderosa pine not just by its thickness but also by its bark color; younger pines tend to be gray-brown while older ones are a cinnamon-red.

North-facing slopes tend to be wet, as they receive less direct exposure from the sun. A mix of Douglas fir, lodgepole pine, ponderosa pine and Engelmann spruce rather than a lone tree species will dominate.

At 1.6 miles, the route arrives at the North Longs Peak Trail junction, about 9768 feet elevation. Go right. The trail then heads through a narrow gorge between East Glacier Knob and 12,668-foot Thatchtop Mountain.

The trail reaches Mills Junction at 2.1 miles. Go left, cross Icy Brook, and officially enter Glacier Gorge.

The streams the trail follows also offer their own unique set of trees. Groves of quaking aspen, willows, mountain alder, and water birch flourish in the wet soil. The aspen is particularly beautiful in autumn when its leaves turn golden-yellow.

At 2.4 miles, the trail reaches the footbridge for Glacier Creek. Look for a footpath on the right; you can follow it for about 40 yards to the base of tiny Glacier Falls.

The montane forest sports an impressive number of mammals and birds. Of the former, various squirrels, chipmunks, cottontails, deer and bobcats call this area home. Among the many songbirds here are the mountain chickadee, western and mountain bluebirds, western tanager, Steller's jay, downy and hairy woodpeckers, and the yellow-rump warbler.

The trail comes upon Mills Lake at 2.65 miles from the trailhead. The subalpine lake, with Half Mountain rising over it, sits at 9955 feet about sea level. It is named for Enos Mills, the father of Rocky Mountain National Park, as he spent several years working to preserve region.

Be sure to bring a picnic basket to enjoy on a rocky area at lake's edge, for the view is fantastic here. To the lake's west is The Arrowhead, which tops out at 12,387 feet, Powell Peak (13,208 feet) and McHenrys Peak (13,327 feet). On the east is while Pagoda Mountain (13,497 feet), the line of pinnacles known as the Keyboard of the Winds. Chiefs Head Peak (13,579 feet) and The Spearhead (12,575 feet) rise in the upper valley.

After taking in the sights, retrace your steps back to the parking lot.

Looking down into Glacier Gorge from Longs Peak.
Mills Lake is the largest lake near the photo's center.

Mountain Lakes

Bear Lake Loop

Day hikers can circle a beautiful subalpine lake in the heart of the national park on the Bear Lake Loop.

The 0.6-miles round trip trail is particularly gorgeous in autumn when aspens around the lake turn gold. An extremely popular trail, it will be crowded during peak tourism season; you can avoid crowds by starting early in morning, usually before 9 a.m.

To reach the trailhead, from Estes Park, take U.S. Hwy. 36 west. Turn left/south onto Bear Lake Road. Drive 9 miles to the parking lot for the Bear Head Trailhead.

From the lot, a short access trail leads to the loop. You're at about 9475 feet elevation, so take the walk slow as there truly is a little less oxygen at this altitude.

Hike the hard-packed surface trail counterclockwise. That follows the 30 marked spots on the trail; an interpretive guide offered by the Rocky Mountain Conservancy explains the history, geology, flora and fauna that can be seen at each numbered posts.

Near the loop's start, along the lake's eastern shore, is a picture-perfect view of Hallett Peak. Its summit sits at 12,713 feet, a full half-mile above the lake. In the morning on clam, clear days, the mountain's reflection can be seen on the lake.

The trail passes through a forest of spruce, fir, lodgepole pine and aspen. The latter only is here because it took root in the aftermath of a great wildfire that take place more than 110 years ago. The "Big Fire" – also sometimes known as the "Bear Lake Fire" because of where it started – burned for eight weeks, reaching temperatures high enough to crack granite boulders. The aspen quickly moved in on the cleared, ash-covered landscape.

In contrast, most of the lodgepole pines around the lake are dead. This has nothing to do with forest fires but a mountain pine beetle infestation that began in the late 1990s following a

Bear Lake

drought. By 2012, the beetle had killed almost all of the mature lodgepole pines in northern Colorado and southern Wyoming.

Still, the views and trail are stunning. As proof, you only

need to reach the lake's north side for the view of Half Mountain, just in front of Longs Peak. The latter rises to 14,259 feet, almost a mile above the lake. Its reflection also can be seen in the lake during clear, calm mornings.

If the majestic views weren't fantastic enough, the simple also will delight hikers on the trail. Watch for the mountain chickadee, which sometimes hangs upside down from branches to pull seeds from pine cones as whistling its sweet song of *fee-bee, fee-bee.*

Upon completing the loop around the lake, take the access trail back to the parking lot.

Other Trails to See Rocky Mountain Lakes

Multiple lakes can be found even at Rocky Mountain National Park's high elevations. Often surrounded by fragrant evergreens with a rising peak reflecting off the crystal blue water, all are beautiful sights to visit. Many of the park's most scenic lakes can be reached via a hike.

Wild Basin Area

• **Lily Lake** – An extremely easy lake to reach, the trailhead starts at the lake off of Colo. Hwy. 7 south of Estes Park. The 0.8-mile wheelchair accessible-trail circles the lake.

• **Ouzel Lake** – The remote lake fills a low spot in a marshy area. From the Wild Basin Trailhead, head west on the trail then go southeast on Thunder Lake Trail then west on Bluebird Trail and lastly south on the spur to the lake for a 10.2-mile round trip.

• **Thunder Lake** – The lake sits below the timber line and is excellent for fishing. Take the same route as for Ouzel Lake except don't turn onto Bluebird Trail for a 13.2-miles round trip journey.

- **Sandbeach Lake** – As the lake's name implies, a sandy beach actually sits on the edge of this lake, a rarity for the mountains. From the Sandbeach Trailhead, take the Sandbeach Lake Trail for a 8.8-miles round trip hike.

Bear Lake area

- **Sprague Lake** – Easy to reach, Sprague is a Rocky Mountain classic with trees reflecting off the surface while a mountain range rises behind it. Take Bear Lake Road west then Sprague Lake Road south; from the parking lot, the 0.9-mile trail circles the lake.
- **Nymph, Dream and Emerald lakes** – All three lakes in Tyndall Gorge can be visited on a 3.6-mile round trip. From the Bear Lake Trailhead, head south from Bear Lake to the Emerald Lake Trail.
- **Lake Hiayaha** – Large boulders surround the lake, which sits at the base of Chaos Canyon. Follow the route to Nymph Lake and once past it go left/south on the Glacier Gorge Trail for a 3.9-mile round trip.

Glacier Gorge Trailhead

- **The Loch, Lake of Glass and Sky Pond** – These three lakes contain populations of hybrid cutthroats (Lake of Glass) and brook trout (Sky Pond). The route runs 5.4-miles round trip from the trailhead on Bear Lake Road.
- **Mills Lake** – This lake can be reached via the Glacier Gorge Trail for a 5.3-mile round trip hike. The lake is filled with rainbow and brook trout.
- **Black Lake** – Past Mills Lake, the Glacier Trail ends at boulder-strewn Black Lake and Ribbon Falls just before it. Brook trout thrive in the lake, which is a 9.6-miles round trip walk.

Fern Lake Trailhead

- **Spruce Lake** – Take the Fern Lake Trail into the forest then turn onto Spruce Lake Trail for a 9.1-mile round trip hike. Primitive unofficial paths lead from it upstream to a pond then Loomis Lake.
- **Fern Lake** – The alpine lake feeds Big Thompson River via Fern Creek, which includes Marguerite Falls. Take the Fern Lake Trail past all three to the lake for a 7.7-miles round trip journey.
- **Odessa Lake** – Continue on the Fern Lake Trail past Fern Lake (9.2 miles round trip) to this waterbody in Tourmaline Gorge. The lake contains rainbow and brook trout.

Lumpy Ridge Trailhead

- **Gem Lake** – The small lake sitting next to a wall of granite is past the Estes Park Overlook. Take stem trail from the trailhead and then the Gem Lake Trail north for a 3.5-miles round trip journey.

Lawn Lake Trailhead

- **Lawn Lake** – In 1982, the earthen dam holding back the lake broke, sending water down Roaring River and killing three people. From the Lawn Lake Trailhead, head north on the Lawn Lake Trail along Roaring River for a 12.5-mile round trip.
- **Crystal Lake** – Hardly a day hike, this beautiful mountain lake is worth the effort if you like backcountry camping. Continue on the Lawn Lake Trail past Lawn Lake for a 14.7-mile round trip.
- **Ypsilon Lake** – The lake sits at the edge of the treeline beneath Ypsilon Mountain. Start on the Lawn Lake Trail then go left/west on the Ypsilon Lake Trail and cross Roaring River for 8.75-miles round trip.

Trail Ridge Road
- **Lake Irene** – A short trail heads to the evergreen-encircled lake on the park's west side. The 0.9-mile trail leaves from the Lake Irene Picnic Area.

Old Fall River Road

Chapin Creek Trail

All too often, national park visitors find themselves limited to the popular sites without easy access to the wild interior. The Old Fall River Road solves that problem for Rocky Mountain National Park visitors.

Built in 1920, the road was the first highway in the park to cross the Continental Divide. While the newer Hwy. 34 is now preferred, park visitors can travel 11 miles on the old route between Horseshoe Park and Fall River Pass.

A great hike to take from the road is the Chapin Creek Trail, which offers opportunities to see moose and elk on a primitive path. It can be hiked about 1.6-miles round trip to the creek crossing or 6.6-miles round trip on a mostly backcountry route to the Poudre Trail.

To reach the trailhead, from Estes Park, take Hwy. 34 – the modern Fall River Road – west into the park. After passing the Sheep Lakes Information Station, turn right/northwest onto Endovalley Road. (If you've crossed Fall River, you've gone too far.)

The paved Endovalley Road becomes Old Fall River Road when the road turns into a one-way, one-lane gravel road, though 2WD vehicles can handle it. With steep drop-offs, tight turns, and no guard rails, the speed limit is 15 mph. It typically is open only July through September.

Built with convict labor during 1915-20, the Old Fall River Road – simply called Fall River Road back then – linked Estes

Park and Grand Lake for the first time. The road hardly was safe by modern standards, with its tight curves and steep drop-offs making for white-knuckled driving.

It was steep as well...so steep that sometimes Model T's backed up the road, as reverse was a lower gear than first gear. Though still dirt, improvements over the decades have make it safer.

About 9 miles from the Hwy. 34 turnoff, the Chapin Creek Trailhead appears on the road's right/north side. Park along the side of the road but be sure to allow enough room for vehicles to pass.

From Chapin Pass, at 11,202 feet, the trail briefly ascends a ridge then through towering evergreens heads down the side of Marmot Point, dropping a couple of hundred feet. Along the way, Chapin Creek rises out of the mountainside, as it begins its course into the valley cut by the creek. At spots where the creek widens, a meadow forms.

Once at the first meadow's edge, start watching for elk and moose. The meadows along the creek are a favorite hangout for them, especially at dusk or during the rutting season.

About 0.8 miles in, the trail crosses to Chapin Creek's west side, paralleling it the rest of the way. This marks a good spot for casual day hikers to turn back.

If continuing on, from there you'll need to make regular use of your navigation skills, as the trail thins and sometimes disappears altogether as crossing downed trees. The key is to simply follow the creek; stay on the west side for drier slopes.

The scenery is magnificent. To the east is the Mummy Range, from which several streams flow into Chapin Creek. The first stream runs off the side of Mount Chapin, whose summit reaches 12,454 feet. A second stream comes off the side of Mount Chiquita, which tops out at 13,069 feet, and Ypsilon Mountain

Chapin Creek Trail

at 13,514 feet. A third stream tumbles down from the Desolation Peaks to the east whose two highest points are just under 13,000 feet. A fourth stream rushes off the north side of Marmot Point, which peaks at 11,909 feet.

When the trail reaches the intersection of Chapin and Cache creeks, it crosses the latter and junctions with the Poudre River Trail. That route continues north along the Cache Poudre River, formed by the merging of the two creeks. This marks the second good spot to turn back.

As driving home, you must continue northwest on Old Fall River Road to the Alpine Visitor Center. From there, you can pick up Hwy. 34 and head back to Estes Park.

Due to heavy snowfall, the road closes in winter.

Other Trails along Old Fall River Road

• **Lawn Lake Trail** – Immediately north of the Hwy. 34 junction, the northern portion of the trail heads to Roaring River and then meets the Ypsilon Trail. The southern route crosses Hwy. 34 and goes to the meadow West Horseshoe Park.

• **Alluvial Fan Trail** – The short hike crosses a spread of rocks and sediment left by Roaring River where it slows before it joins the Fork River. An east and a west trailhead are along the road.

• **Chasm Falls Trail** – Literally less than a hundred feet in length, the trail heads from a parking lot alongside the road to the Fall River waterfall. The rock here funnels the water into a narrow gorge where it drops 25 feet.

• **Alpine Ridge Trail** – After crossing alpine tundra, the road ends at the Alpine Visitor Center and rejoins Hwy. 34. This trail can be taken to a point 300 feet above the center.

Alpine Tundra
Alpine Ridge Trail

If you're looking to prove your mettle, you may want to hike one of Rocky Mountain National Park's shortest trails.

The 0.6-mile round trip gains 300 feet while sitting at an altitude of 12,000 feet above sea level, where there's significantly less oxygen than most of us are used to. Because of that, the route through the alpine tundra appropriately is nicknamed Huffer's Hill. Your reward? Panoramic vistas and tiny wildflowers...oh, and self-pride in knowing you did one of the toughest day hikes around.

To reach the trailhead, take U.S. Hwy. 34/Trail Ridge Road to Fall River Pass. Use the parking lot for the Alpine Visitor Center. For the more adventurous, the Old Fall River Road also leads to the visitor center. Both highways close during winter, usually mid-October to May.

The trailhead is at the eastern end of the parking lot where Old Fall River Road enters it. You're at 11,796 feet elevation.

Much of the trail's surface is either paved or a series of rock slabs that form a staircase across the tundra.

Vibrant ecosystem

The park's alpine tundra is a harsh environment that begins

Alpine Ridge Trail

where the treeline ends at about 11,000 feet above sea level. About a third of the park sits in the ecosystem.

Because of the rocky surface and extreme cold, plants growing here are diminutive. The majority are perennials while lichen clings to rocks. Still, about 200 species of grasses, forbs and mosses thrive there.

This open meadow makes a great feeding ground for elk, and you're likely to spot a few of them grazing or resting as you walk. Most of the other mammals here are far smaller, however, and you may be lucky enough to spot a chipmunk, snowshoe hare, gopher or a yellow-bellied marmot.

The trail's destination is the top of an unnamed nob that offers 360 degree views of the surrounding area, including the pass to the southeast. To the east is another nob, known as Marmot Point. The Never Summer Mountains rise in the west.

When done taking in the sites, retrace your steps back to the parking lot. The visitor center offers displays about the tundra, a small ranger station, gift shop/bookstore, bathrooms, and a small snack shop.

If a thunderstorm is approaching, skip the trail. As you're above the treeline, you'll be among the highest objects on the ground and a prime target for lightning.

Night skies

The best places to see the Northern Lights and the night sky in Rocky Mountain National Park is just about anywhere away from the urbanized edge of the Front Range or near Grand Lake. The glow of man-made lights diminishes the number of stars and anything else that can be seen in the night sky.

Alpine tundras far from visitor centers or campgrounds are ideal, as there are no man-made lights or treeline to obscure views. Sundance Mountain and the Mushroom Rocks along Trail Ridge Road are two such areas. Always face away from the highway so that headlights from passing vehicles don't temporarily blind you.

From mid-June through mid-July, the park offers a variety of astronomy-oriented activities. They include Party with the Stars, Astronomy in the Park and the Rocky Mountain National Park Night Sky Festival.

If visiting the park in August, drive to the top of Trail Ridge Road to watch the annual Perseid meteor shower. The shower consists of debris and dust, left by a passing comet, which burn up in the atmosphere as falling to the ground. The peak shower usually is Aug. 11-13.

Other Trails to See Rocky Mountain Alpine Terrain

With so many of the national park's mountains above the

tree line, there is plenty of alpine tundra to explore. A couple of those areas and the trails that will get you there include:

- **Flattop Mountain** – The rocky summit of Flaptop Mountain sits at 12,324 feet. To reach the tundra, from the Bear Lake Trailhead hike the east side of Bear Lake then go right/east onto the Bear Lake Trail; next turn left/west onto the Flat Top Trail.
- **Trail Ridge** – For centuries, Arapaho and Ute Indians walked this tundra route between their winter and summer hunting grounds. The 4.0-mile one-way Ute Trail follows part of this ancient journey; the trailhead is off of U.S. Hwy 34 between the Rainbow Curve Outlook and the Forest Canyon Overlook.

Continental Divide

Milner Pass Trail

Day hikers can place their feet on both side of the Continental Divide when hiking the Milner Pass Trail.

The 4.1-mile one-way trail makes for a long round-trip hike, but the route can be shortened or treated as a shuttle trail. Because of the high elevation, the road to the trailhead often is closed in winter, so July through September is the narrow window hikers have to hit this route.

To reach the trailhead, from Estes Park drive west on U.S. Hwy. 34/Trail Ridge Road. Park at the Poudre Lake Trailhead at Milner Pass, which sits 10,759 feet above sea level.

Before beginning the hike, walk the fenced path northeast to Poudre Lake. The lake is the headwaters of the Cache La Poudre River that flows east into the Platte River.

The Continental Divide runs across two continents from the Bering Strait to the Strait of Magellan. All water west of the divide ultimately drains into the Pacific Ocean while water east

Poudre Lake on Milner Pass Trail

of it heads into the Atlantic Ocean, Gulf of Mexico and Caribbean Sea. At Milner Pass, the divide is southwest of the Poudre Lake shore and marked by a large sign. The Milner Pass Trail crosses the Divide three times.

From the parking lot, head south on the narrow but obvious trail that cuts through the grass and evergreens. The route is initially steep as it passes Sheep Rock, which is on the Divide's Pacific side. After a hairpin turn, the trail gradually veers northeast, recrossing the Divide to its Atlantic side.

At 0.6 miles, the trail reaches a junction with an unmaintained path to Mt. Ida. Continue heading straight/northwest. The terrain quickly levels out as the trail heads through thinning patches of subalpine forest the rest of the way.

In the meadows, Specimen Mountain, at more than 12,400 feet, towers over the north and west side of the Cache La Poudre River. To the south and east are twin 11,880-foot peaks, which Poudre Lake sits at the base of.

Bring a binoculars. Elk and deer often can be spotted in the middle portion of the hike. Bighorn sheep also sometimes can be seen on the mountain slopes while moose sometimes feed in the alpine ponds and meadows.

At two miles from the trailhead, the route reaches Forest Canyon Pass. Widening to the southeast, the canyon is where the headwaters of the Big Thompson River forms.

Several scenic ponds dot the flats. But at Forest Canyon Pass, perhaps the most impressive view requires you to pause and turn around. Never Summer Ridge is now visible in the west. Ten distinct peaks top out at above 12,000 feet in the range.

About three miles from the trailhead, breaks in the treeline allow views of Cache La Poudre River to the north. The trail soon splits; the route on the right heads to Gore Range Overlook, while going left/northeast is the Milner Pass Trail.

For the last 0.6 miles, the trail largely crosses open tundra on a west-facing slope. The grade increases here but is fairly moderate.

About 4.1 miles from Milner Pass, the trail arrives at Alpine Visitor Center. The elevation at the center, which sits along Trail Ridge Road at Fall River Pass, is 11,796 feet.

With these high elevations throughout the trail, always pace yourself and drink plenty of water. Be on constant alert for altitude sickness.

Sometimes this route is referred to as Ute Trail on maps. It technically is part of that trail, of which two disconnected sections exist in the national park.

Trail Ridge Road
Colorado River Trail

The best way to see the heart of Rocky Mountain National Park is a drive along the famous Trail Ridge Road, a 48-mile section of U.S. Hwy. 34 running from Estes Park to Grand Lake. Designed in the 1930s to sweep across the landscape to give grand views of the mountains, drivers gain elevation on it via long continuous curves. Plenty of turnouts to enjoy fantastic vistas – as well as many trailheads to explore those sights up close – can be found along the highway.

Among the best of the latter is the Colorado River trailhead, which is open year-round on a highway that often closes mid-October through May thanks to heavy snowfall.

Known as the "Highway to the Sky," 10 miles of the Trail Ridge Road runs above 11,000 feet. It is one of the world's highest paved roads.

Another long section of the highway parallels the beautiful Colorado River. To reach the Colorado River trailhead from Trail Ridge Road, turn west into the marked parking lot for the trailhead, which is closer to Grand Lake than Estes Park.

From there, take the Colorado River Trail to the ruins of an 19th century mining town, Lulu City, in a 6.2-miles round trip with 320-foot elevation gain. The trail leaves from the lot's north side at 9040 feet above sea level.

Crossing a thick rolling woodland, the trail offers nice views of Colorado River, arguably the Southwest's most important waterway. The trail runs in the same direction as the river but never comes within more than 100 feet of it. If the river looks a bit small, that's because you're very close to its source, which is La Poudre Pass Lake just 6.5 miles from the trailhead.

Grassy meadows can be found along the way. It's the perfect environment for elk to graze and then hide in the woods, and you'll likely see some of the large hoofed mammals here. Be sure to remain clear of them, especially if they pull their ears back or make any threatening gestures, which is a sign that a calf is nearby.

Lulu City at Colorado River Trail

In addition to the river and elk, lining the horizon to the west is the Never Summer Mountains range. Though a small range, it's quite tall with ten peaks rising above 12,000 feet. Having formed a mere 24-29 million years ago, they're also much younger than the surrounding Rockies, which rose 55-88 million years ago.

Closer to the trail, dusky grouse often can be seen feeding on seeds and raspberries in the brush, especially near conifers. The bird has the interesting habit of moving to higher elevations during winter where it feeds on evergreen needles.

The first man-made site along the way is the ruins of the Shipler mine on a talus slop just above the trail. A few yards later is the Shipler cabin, a set of stacked logs in a small clearing.

About three miles from the trailhead, the route turns sharply right and begins to climb steeply. Watch closely for the narrow stem trail that runs to Lulu City, and take it left. The path drops about 100 feet in elevation before arriving at the ruins.

From 1879-84, Lulu City was a gold, silver and lead mining town with a population of about 200.

At that time, 40 cabins, several sawmills, a hotel, a justice of the peace, and a stagecoach service (with rides to and from Fort Collins three times a week) filled this area. As the silver turned out to be low grade, the cost of transporting it simply wasn't worth it, and the site soon was abandoned. All that remains of Lulu City today are a few log cabin planks and a modern albeit rustic sign marking the location.

Upon taking in the ruins, retrace your steps back to the parking lot.

Note: Some maps refer to this as La Poudre Pass Trail. If continuing the hike behind the turnoff to Lulu City, the trail heads to that pass and the Colorado River's source.

Other Trails along Trail Ridge Road

Note that Hwy. 34 is known as Fall River Road from Estes Park west to the U.S. Hwy 36 intersection at Deer Ridge Junction. Heading east to west, the trails include:

• **Lawn Lake Trail** – The trailhead sits just north of Hwy. 34 off of Endovalley Road. Heading south, the trail crosses the Fall River and enters the meadow West Horseshoe Park. Going north, the trail runs to Roaring River near Horseshoe Falls.

• **Ute Trail (Deer Ridge section)** – At Deer Ridge Junction, go left/east onto U.S. Hwy. 36. The Ute Trail heads south from the Deer Junction Trailhead on its way to Upper Beaver Meadows.

• **Ute Trail (Trail Ridge section)** – This route, used by Native Americans to reach summer hunting grounds, crosses an alpine tundra. Park in a pull-off along the road's south side.

• **Forest Canyon Overlook Trail** – A short trail cuts across the alpine tundra to a vista of a forest in the valley below. The parking lot is less than a mile from the Ute Trail trailhead.

• **Mushroom Rocks Trail** – A small trail heads to some interesting rock formations. Parking is in a pullout on the road's south side, so be careful when crossing the highway.

• **Toll Memorial Trail** – The trail heads over an alpine tundra and past the Mushroom Rocks formation. It ends at sister rock outcroppings just beyond the Mushroom Rocks.

• **Ute Trail (Fall River Pass section)** – At the Fall River Pass, the trail goes west and downhill over more alpine tundra to the evergreen Forest Canyon Pass. Park in the lot for the Alpine Visitor Center.

• **Alpine Ridge Trail** – The route heads a mere 0.3 miles from the Alpine Visitor Center up 300 feet through an alpine tundra to the summit of Huffer's Hill. Because of the altitude – 12,000 feet above sea level – it'll probably be the toughest third of a mile you've ever walked.

• **Poudre River Trail** – After descending the ridge from the Alpine Visitor Center, this trail heads north through evergreens. It parallels the Cache la Poudre River.

• **Milner Pass Trail** – The route, a segment of the Ute Trail, crosses the Continental Divide, as it heads north from the Poudre Lake Trailhead toward the alpine tundra. It can be taken all the way to the Alpine Visitor Center.

• **Lake Irene Trail** – A short trail runs to pretty Lake Irene, which is surrounded by evergreens. The trail leaves from the Lake Irene Picnic Area.

• **Timber Lake Trail** – The trail heads south across Beaver Creek through an alpine forest to Timber Creek. The lot is on the road's east side across from the Colorado River Trailhead.

• **Holzwarth Trail** – The trail – unpaved Ditch Road – crosses the Colorado River and ends at the Holzwarth Historic Site. To find the parking lot, watch for the sign announcing the historic site.

• **Bowen/Baker Trail** – The sand road crosses the Colorado River and a meadow then enters the forest. Baker Trail splits north, paralleling a creek through Barker Gulch then curving around Baker Mountain to a mountain pass. Bowen Trail heads south to Gaskill Cemetery in Bowen Gulch.

• **Coyote Valley Trail** – The trail runs north-south alongside the Colorado River. An expansive meadow sits west of the path.

• **Onahu Creek Trail** – The route heads north from the trailhead to Onahu Creek and splits with one route heading back to a point farther north on the highway and the other eastward alongside the creek. It also goes south to the Green Mountain Trail.

• **Green Mountain Trail** – Going west on the trail leads hikers through a forest beneath Green Mountain to a meadow surrounding Tonahutu Creek. Crossing the highway to the eastern portion of the trail loops through woods past Harbison Meadows.

• **Kawuneeche Visitor Center Trail** – From the Kawuneeche Visitor Center, the trail goes east into the forests alongside Harbison Ditch. Crossing the highway, it connects with the Green Mountain Trail.

Other Trails to See Rocky Mountain National Park History

From mining to cattle ranching, Rocky Mountain National Park enjoys a fascinating history, some of which is preserved via buildings, ruins and trails. A good sampling of those historic areas include:

• **McGraw Ranch** – The working cattle ranch operated near

Estes Park from 1884 to 1948. Many structures, including the barn and corral from 1884, still stand. It can be reached via the Cow Creek Trailhead in a 0.33-miles walk.

• **Utility Area Historic District** – Buildings in this area reflect the national parks' rustic design popular when they were built in the 1920s and 1930s. Some were constructed by the Civilian Conservation Corps. The area is off of the Park Entrance Road west of Marys Lake Road.

• **Ute Trail** – Arapaho and Ute Indians for centuries crossed Trail Ridge as one of their routes to reach their summer hunting grounds on the Great Plains. This area off of U.S. Hwy. 34 is alpine tundra.

• **Holzwarth Trail** – A historic ranch started by a German immigrant in the 1910s is preserved on the park's west side in the Kawuneeche Valley. It can be reached by hiking unpaved Ditch Road, which crosses the Colorado River and ends at the historic site.

• **Gaskill Cemetery** – About all that remains of the 1880s mining town of Gaskill is its cemetery. It can be reached via Bowen Trail, a sand road, which crosses the Colorado then heads south to Gaskill Cemetery in Bowen Gulch on a 6-miles round trip hike.

Mountain Meadows
Adams Falls Trail

Day hikers can enjoy a picturesque mountain meadow after passing a 55-foot waterfall on the Adams Falls Trail.

The 0.9-miles round trip is an easy walk on the park's west side. Autumn marks a great time to hike the trail as aspen leaves have turned a brilliant yellow, though the waterflow at the falls will be low compared to May when at its peak.

To reach the trailhead, from Grand Lake take West Portal

Road east/south to the East Inlet parking lot. This is the national park's West Portal. Because the trail starts outside of the park's boundaries, there are no entrance fees.

The East Inlet Trailhead begins at the lot's southeast corner. The National Park Service and the Civilian Conservation Corps constructed the trail using rock, wood and dirt from the local area. There is a neat wood fence at the trailhead and impressive masonry near the falls.

The elevation is 8390 feet above sea level, so though the trail is easy, take your time. There really is less oxygen this high up, and altitude sickness can set in for those not acclimated.

Fortunately, the trail instantly relaxes you as it heads uphill through fragrant pines mixed with aspen. After entering the park, about a third of a mile from the trailhead, you'll reach a side trail that goes to the waterfalls. Turn right/south onto the new trail.

In short order, you'll come to an overlook of the picturesque falls, which drops 55 feet over several steps on East Inlet Creek. The falls is named for Jay Adams, one of the first white settlers of the Grand Lake area in the 1800s; it previously was called Ousel Falls.

From the overlook, the trail runs to the top of the falls. This vista not only gives another great view of the falls but the waterbody Grand Lake to the northwest.

The trail next goes north and rejoins the East Inlet Trail. From there, turn left/west, heading back to the parking lot.

If you have some extra energy, though, instead go right/east. In a half-mile, you'll reach the point where East Inlet and Echo creeks merge. A large meadow with wildflowers – and sometimes even moose – can be found there.

Among the most pleasant scenes at Rocky Mountain Nation-

Adams Falls Trail

al Park are the many montane meadows. Generally found in valleys between 5600-9500 feet elevation, these grass-dominated sections of the valleys usually are too wet or too dry for trees to grow.

The grasses and forbs in these meadows provide food and habitat for an incredible number of animals. In fact, if you want to spot wildlife at the park, the meadows are a great place to do so.

Rocky Mountain's meadows attract elk, deer, both Wyoming and golden mantled ground squirrels, as well as a variety of migrating birds and insects. Several animals use the meadows seasonally as winter buries their mountainside homes in snow. Among them are bighorn sheep, black bear, and mountain lion.

Locally called "parks," these meadows typically formed when glacial lakes drained at the end of the last ice age. This can leave many meadows with sandy topsoil and a generally flat terrain.

Moose occasionally appeared in northern Colorado during the late 1800s then disappeared. The Colorado Division of Wildlife recently reintroduced them to the park.

The hike from the parking lot Adams Falls to the creeks' confluence runs 1.9-miles round trip.

Other Trails to See Rocky Mountain Meadows

Several scenic mountain meadows, full of wildlife and wildflowers, can be found in the national park. Most of these can be reached via a day hike:

• **Big Meadows** – The largest montane meadow in the park, it's an excellent place to spot moose, elk and deer grazing in the grass or the fen. The 3.6-mile round trip Green Mountain Trail heads to a clump of boulders at the meadows' edge. The path is a segment of the Continental Divide National Scenic Trail.

• **Long Meadows** – Stretching two miles between Timber and Onahu creeks, this is an isolated meadow. Small streams in the meadow create a small marshy area. The Timber Lake Trail runs 7.6-miles round trip primarily through forests to the meadow.

- **Upper Beaver Meadows** – This broad meadow offers great views of Longs Peak and mountains on the Continental Divide. The 5-mile Upper Beaver Meadows Loop circles and also cuts through the grassland. Hike the trail clockwise.

- **Hollowell Park** – This large and marshy meadow along Mill Creek is known for moose and packs a lot of local history. Ranchers and sawmills could be found in the area through the early 1900s. The Hollowell Park Trail runs 2.75-miles round trip to Mill Creek Basin.

- **Shipler Park** – A small meadow sits along the Colorado River at the base of Shipler Mountain. The La Poudre Pass Trail crosses the meadows on the way to the historical mining ruins of Lulu City, which is 3.1 miles from the Colorado River trailhead.

- **Kawuneeche Valley** – A large meadow fills this area, whose name comes from the Arapaho word meaning "valley of the coyote." The aptly-named Coyote Valley Trail runs through part of the meadow. Visit in spring when an array of wildflowers bloom.

Bonus Section:
Day Hiking Primer

Y ou'll get more out of a day hike if you research it and plan ahead. It's not enough to just pull over to the side of the road and hit a trail that you've never been on and have no idea where it goes. In fact, doing so invites disaster.

Instead, you should preselect a trail (This book's trail descriptions can help you do that). You'll also want to ensure that you have the proper clothing, equipment, navigational tools, first-aid kit, food and water. Knowing the rules of the trail and potential dangers along the way also are helpful. In this special section, we'll look at each of these topics to ensure you're fully prepared.

Selecting a Trail

For your first few hikes, stick to short, well-known trails where you're likely to encounter others. Once you get a feel for hiking, your abilities, and your interests, expand to longer and more remote trails.

Always check to see what the weather will be like on the trail you plan to hike. While an adult might be able to withstand wind and a sprinkle here or there, for kids it can be pure misery. Dry, pleasantly warm days with limited wind always are best when hiking with children.

Don't choose a trail that is any longer than the least fit person in your group can hike. Adults in good shape can go 8-

12 miles a day; for kids, it's much less. There's no magical number.

When planning the hike, try to find a trail with a mid-point payoff – that is something you and definitely any children will find exciting about half-way through the hike. This will help keep up everyone's energy and enthusiasm during the journey.

If you have children in your hiking party, consider a couple of additional points when selecting a trail.

Until children enter their late teens, they need to stick to trails rather than going off-trail hiking, which is known as bushwhacking. Children too easily can get lost when off trail. They also can easily get scratched and cut up or stumble across poisonous plants and dangerous animals.

Generally, kids will prefer a circular route to one that requires hiking back the way you came. The return trip often feels anti-climatic, but you can overcome that by mentioning features that all of you might want to take a closer look at.

Once you select a trail, it's time to plan for your day hike. Doing so will save you a lot of grief – and potentially prevent an emergency. You are, after all, entering the wilds, a place where help may not be readily available.

When planning your hike, follow these steps:

• Print a road map showing how to reach the parking lot near the trailhead. Outline the route with a transparent yellow highlighter and write out the directions.

• Print a satellite photo of the parking area and the trailhead. Mark the trailhead on the photo.

• Print a topo map of the trail. Outline the trail with the yellow highlighter. Note interesting features you want to see along the trail and the destination.

• If carrying GPS, program this information into your device.

• Make a timeline for your trip, listing: when you will leave home; when you will arrive at the trailhead; your turn back time; when you will return for home in your vehicle; and when you will arrive at your home.

• Estimate how much water and food you will need to bring based on the amount of time you plan to spend on the trail and in your vehicle. You'll need at least two pints of water per person for every hour on the trail.

• Fill out two copies of a hiker's safety form. Leave one in your vehicle.

• Share all of this information with a responsible person remaining in civilization, leaving a hiker's safety form with them. If they do not hear from you within an hour of when you plan to leave the trail in your vehicle, they should contact authorities to report you as possibly lost.

Clothing
Footwear

If your feet hurt, the hike is over, so getting the right footwear is worth the time. Making sure the footwear fits before hitting the trail also is a good idea. With children, if you've gone a few weeks without hiking, that's plenty of time for feet to grow, and they may have just outgrown their hiking boots. Check out everyone's footwear a few days before head-ing out on the hike. If it doesn't fit, replace it.

For flat, smooth, dry trails, sneakers and cross-trainers are fine, but if you really want to head onto less traveled roads or tackle areas that aren't typically dry, you'll need hiking boots. Once you start doing any rocky or steep trails – and remember that a trail you consider moderately steep needs to be only half that angle for a child to consider it extremely steep – you'll want hiking boots, which offer rugged tread perfect for handling rough trails.

Socks

Socks serve two purposes: to wick sweat away from skin and to provide cushioning. Cotton socks aren't very good for hiking, except in extremely dry environments, because they retain moisture that can lead to blisters. Wool socks or liner socks work best. You'll want to look for three-season socks, also known as trekking socks. While a little thicker than summer socks, their extra cushioning generally prevents blisters. Also, make sure kids don't put on holey socks; that's just inviting blisters.

Layering

On all but hot, dry days, when hiking you should wear multiple layers of clothing that provide various levels of protection against sweat, heat loss, wind and potentially rain. Layering works because the type of clothing you select for each stratum serves a different function, such as wicking moisture or shielding against wind. In addition, trapped air between each layer of clothing is warmed by your body heat. Layers also can be added or taken off as needed.

Generally, you need three layers. Closest to your skin is the wicking layer, which pulls perspiration away from the body and into the next layer, where it evaporates. Exertion from walking means you will sweat and generate heat, even if the weather is cold. The second layer provides insulation, which helps keep you warm. The last layer is a water-resistant shell that protects you from rain, wind, snow and sleet.

As the seasons and weather change, so does the type of clothing you select for each layer. The first layer ought to be a loose-fitting T-shirt in summer, but in winter and on other cold days you might opt for a long-sleeved moisture-wicking synthetic material, like polypropylene. During winter, the next layer probably also should cover the neck, which often is exposed to the elements. A turtleneck works fine, but preferably not one made of cotton. The third layer in winter, depending on the temperature, could be a wool sweater, a half-zippered long sleeved fleece jacket, or a fleece vest.

You might even add a fourth layer of a hooded parka with pockets, made of material that can block wind and resist water. Gloves or mittens as well as a hat also are necessary on cold days.

Headgear

Half of all body heat is lost through the head, hence the hiker's adage, "If your hands are cold, wear a hat." In cool, wet weather, wearing a hat is at least good for avoiding hypothermia, a potentially deadly condition in which heat loss occurs faster than the body can generate it. Children are more susceptible to hypothermia than adults.

Especially during summer, a hat with a wide brim is useful in keeping the sun out of eyes. It's also nice should rain start falling.

For young children, get a hat with a chin strap. They like to play with their hats, which will fly off in a wind gust if not fastened some way to the child.

Sunglasses

Sunglasses are an absolute must if walking through open areas exposed to the sun and in winter when you can suffer from snow blindness. Look for 100% UV-protective shades, which provide the best screen.

Equipment

A couple of principles should guide your purchases. First,

the longer and more complex the hike, the more equipment you'll need. Secondly, your general goal is to go light. Since you're on a day hike, the amount of gear you'll need is a fraction of what backpackers shown in magazines and catalogues usually carry. Still, the inclination of most day hikers is to not carry enough equipment. For the lightness issue, most gear today is made with titanium and siliconized nylon, ensuring it is sturdy yet fairly light. While the following list of what you need may look long, it won't weigh much.

Backpacks

Sometimes called daypacks (for day hikes or for kids), backpacks are essential to carry all of the essentials you need – snacks, first-aid kit, extra clothing.

For day hiking, you'll want to get yourself an internal frame, in which the frame giving the backpack its shape is inside the pack's fabric so it's not exposed to nature. Such frames usually are lightweight and comfortable. External frames have the frame outside the pack, so they are exposed to the elements. They are excellent for long hikes into the backcountry when you must carry heavy loads.

As kids get older, and especially after they've been hiking for a couple of years, they'll want a "real" backpack. Unfortunately, most backpacks for kids are overbuilt and too heavy. Even light ones that safely can hold up to 50 pounds are inane for most children.

When buying a daypack for your child, look for sternum straps, which help keep the strap on the shoulders. This is vital for prepubescent children, as they do not have the broad shoulders that come with adolescence, meaning packs likely will slip off and onto their arms, making them uncomfortable and difficult to carry. Don't buy a backpack that a child will "grow into." Backpacks that don't fit well simply will lead to sore shoulder and back muscles and could result in poor posture.

Also, consider purchasing a daypack with a hydration system for kids. This will help ensure they drink a lot of water. More on this later when we get to canteens.

Before hitting the trail, always check your children's backpacks to make sure that they have not overloaded them. Kids think they need more than they really do. They also tend to overestimate their own ability to carry stuff. Sibling rivalries often lead to children packing more than they should in their rucksacks, too. Don't let them overpack "to teach them a lesson," though, as it can damage bones and turn the hike into a bad experience.

A good rule of thumb is no more than 25 percent capacity. Most upper elementary school kids can carry only about 10 pounds for any short distance. Subtract the weight of the backpack, and that means only 4-5 pounds in the backpack. Overweight children will need to carry a little less than this or they'll quickly be out of breath.

Child carriers

You'll have to carry infant and toddlers. Until infants can hold their heads up, which usually doesn't happen until about four to six months of age, a front pack (like a Snugli or Baby Bjorn) is best. It keeps the infant close for warmth and balances out your backpack. At the same time, though, you must watch for baby overheating in a front pack, so you'll need to remove the infant from your body at rest stops.

Once children reach about 20 pounds, they typically can hold their heads up and sit on their own. At that point, you'll want a baby carrier (sometimes called a child carrier or baby backpack), which can transfer the infant's weight to your hips when you walk. You'll not only be comfortable, but your child will love it, too.

Look for a baby carrier that is sturdy yet lightweight. Your child is going to get heavier as time passes, so about the only way you can counteract this is to reduce the weight of the items you use to carry things. The carrier also should have adjustment points, as you don't want your child to outgrow the carrier too soon. A padded waist belt and padded shoulder straps are necessary for your comfort. The carrier should provide some kind of head and neck support if you're hauling an infant. It also should offer back support for children of all ages, and leg holes should be wide enough so there's no chafing. You want to be able to load your infant without help, so it should be stable enough to stand that way when you take it off the child can sit in it for a moment while you get turned around. Stay away from baby carriers with only shoulder straps as you need the waist belt to help shift the child's weight to your hips for more comfortable walking.

Fanny packs

Also known as a belt bag, a fanny pack is virtually a must for anyone with a baby carrier, as you can't otherwise lug a backpack. If your significant other is with you, he or she can carry the backpack, of course. Still, the fanny pack also is a good alternative to a backpack in hot weather, as it will reduce back sweat.

If you have only one or two kids on a hike, or if they also are old enough to carry daypacks, your fanny pack need not be large. A mid-size pouch can carry at least 200 cubic inches of supplies, which is more than enough to accommodate all the materials you need. A good fanny pack also has a spot for hooking canteens to.

Canteens

Canteens or plastic bottles filled with water are vital for any hike, no matter how short the trail. You'll need to have enough of them to carry about two pints of water per person for every hour of hiking.

Trekking poles

Also known as walking poles or walking sticks, trekking poles are necessary for maintaining stability on uneven or wet surfaces and to help reduce fatigue. The latter makes them useful on even surfaces. By transferring weight to the arms, a trekking pole can reduce stress on your knees and lower back, allowing you to maintain a better posture and to go farther.

If an adult with a baby or toddler on your back, you'll primarily want a trekking pole to help you maintain your balance, even if on a flat surface, and to help absorb some of the impact of your step.

Graphite tips provide the best traction. A basket just above the tip is a good idea so the stick doesn't sink into mud or sand. Angled cork handles are ergonomic and help absorb sweat from your hands so they don't blister. A strap on the handle to wrap around your hand is useful so the stick doesn't slip out. Telescopic poles are a good idea as you can adjust them as needed based on the terrain you're hiking and as kids grow to accommodate their height.

The pole also needs to be sturdy enough to handle rugged terrain, as you don't want a pole that bends when you press it to the ground. Spring-loaded shock absorbers help when heading down a steep incline but aren't necessary. Indeed, for a short walk across flat terrain, the right length stick is about all you need.

Carabiners

Carabiners are metal loops, vaguely shaped like a D, with a sprung or screwed gate. You'll find that hooking a couple of them to your backpack or fanny pack useful in many ways. For example, if you need to dig through a fanny pack, you can hook the strap of your trekking pole to it. Your hat, camera straps, first-aid kit, and a number of other objects also can connect to them. Hook carabiners to your fanny pack or backpack upon purchasing them so you don't forget them when packing. Small carabiners with sprung gates are inexpensive, but they do have a limited life span of a couple of dozen hikes.

Navigational Tools

Paper maps

Paper maps may sound passé in this age of GPS, but you'll find the variety and breadth of view they offer to be useful. During the planning process, a paper map (even if viewing it online), will be far superior to a GPS device. On the hike, you'll also want a backup to GPS. Or like many casual hikers, you may not own GPS at all, which makes paper maps indispensable.

Standard road maps (which includes printed guides and handmade trail maps) show highways and locations of cities and parks. Maps included in guidebooks, printed guides handed out at parks, and those that are hand-drawn tend to be designed like road maps, and often carry the same positives and negatives.

Topographical maps give contour lines and other important details for crossing a landscape. You'll find them invaluable on a hike into the wilds. The contour lines' shape and their spacing on a topo map show the form and steepness of a hill or bluff, unlike the standard road map and most brochures and hand-drawn trail maps. You'll also know if you're in a woods, which is marked in green, or in a clearing, which is marked in white. If you get lost, figuring out where you are and how to get to where you need to be will be much easier with such information.

Aerial photos offer a view from above that is rendered exactly as it would look from an airplane. Thanks to Google and other online services, you can get fairly detailed pictures of the landscape. Such pictures are an excellent resource when researching a hiking trail. Unfortunately, those pictures don't label what a feature is or what it's called, as would a topo map. Unless there's a stream, determining if a feature is a valley bottom or a ridgeline also can be difficult. Like topo maps, satellite and aerial photos can be out of date a few years.

GPS

By using satellites, the global positioning system can find your spot on the Earth to within 10 feet. With a GPS device, you can preprogram the trailhead location and mark key turns and landmarks as well as the hike's end point. This mobile map is a powerful technological tool that almost certainly ensures you won't get lost – so long as you've correctly programmed the information. GPS also can calculate travel time and act as a compass, a barometer and altimeter, making such devices virtually obsolete on a hike.

In remote areas, however, reception is spotty at best for GPS, rendering your mobile map worthless. A GPS device also runs on batteries, and there's always a chance they will go dead. Or you may drop your device, breaking it in the process. Their screens are small, and sometimes you need a large paper map to get a good sense of the natural landmarks around you.

Compass

Like a paper map, a compass is indispensable even if you use GPS. Should your GPS no longer function, the compass then can be used to tell you which direction you're heading. A protractor compass is best for hiking. Beneath the compass needle is a transparent base with lines to help your orient yourself. The compass often serves as a magnifying glass to help you make out map details. Most protractor compasses also come with a lanyard for easy carrying.

Food and Water

Water

As water is the heaviest item you'll probably carry, there is a temptation to not take as much as one should. Don't skimp on the amount of water you bring, though; after all, it's the one supply your body most needs. It's always better to end up having more water than needed than returning to your vehicle dehydrated.

How much water should you take? Adults need at least a quart for every two hours hiking. Children need to drink about a quart every two hours of walking and more if the weather is hot or dry. To keep kids hydrated, have them drink at every rest stop.

Don't presume there will be water on the hiking trail. Most trails outside of urban areas lack such an amenity. In addition, don't drink water from local streams, lakes, rivers or ponds. There's no way to tell if local water is safe or not. As soon as you have consumed half of your water supply, you should turn around for the vehicle.

Food

Among the many wonderful things about hiking is that

snacking between meals isn't frowned upon. Unless going on an all-day hike in which you'll picnic along the way, you want to keep everyone in your hiking party fed, especially as hunger can lead to lethargic and discontented children. It'll also keep young kids from snacking on the local flora or dirt. Before hitting the trail, you'll want to repackage as much of the food as possible as products sold at grocery stores tend to come in bulky packages that take up space and add a little weight to your backpack. Place the food in re-sealable plastic bags.

Bring a variety of small snacks for rest stops. You don't want kids filling up on snacks, but you do need them to maintain their energy levels if they're walking or to ensure they don't turn fussy if riding in a child carrier. Go for complex carbo-hy-drates and proteins for maintaining energy. Good options in-clude dried fruits, jerky, nuts, peanut butter, prepared energy bars, candy bars with a high protein content (nuts, peanut but-ter), crackers, raisins and trail mix (called "gorp"). A num-ber of trail mix recipes are available online; you and your child-ren may want to try them out at home to see which ones you col-lectively like most.

Salty treats rehydrate better than sweet treats do. Chocolate and other sweets are fine if they're not all that's served, but re-member they also tend to lead to thirst and to make sticky messes. Whichever snacks you choose, don't experiment with food on the trail. Bring what you know kids will like.

Give the first snack within a half-hour of leaving the trailhead or you risk children becoming tired and whiny from low energy levels. If kids start asking for them every few steps even after having something to eat at the last rest stop, consider timing snacks to reaching a seeable landmark, such as, "We'll get out the trail mix when we reach that bend up ahead."

Milk for infants

If you have an infant or unweaned toddler with you, milk is as necessary as water. Children who only drink breastfed milk but don't have their mother on the hike require that you have breast-pumped milk in an insulated beverage container (such as a Thermos) that can keep it cool to avoid spoiling. Know how much the child drinks and at what frequency so you can bring enough. You'll also need to carry the child's bottle and feeding nipples. Bring enough extra water in your canteen so you can wash out the bottle after each feeding. A handkerchief can be used to dry bottles between feedings.

Don't forget the baby's pacifier. Make sure it has a string and hook attached so it connects to the baby's outfit and isn't lost.

What not to bring

Avoid soda and other caffeinated beverages, alcohol, and energy pills. The caffeine will dehydrate children as well as you. Alcohol has no place on the trail; you need your full faculties when making decisions and driving home. Energy pills essentially are a stimulant and like alcohol can lead to bad calls. If you're tired, get some sleep and hit the trail another day.

First-aid Kit

After water, this is the most essential item you can carry.

A first-aid kit should include:

- Adhesive bandages of various types and sizes, especially butterfly bandages (for younger kids, make sure they're colorful kid bandages)
- Aloe vera
- Anesthetic (such as Benzocaine)
- Antacid (tablets)

- Antibacterial (aka antibiotic) ointment (such as Neosporin or Bacitracin)
- Anti-diarrheal tablets (for adults only, as giving this to a child is controversial)
- Anti-itch cream or calamine lotion
- Antiseptics (such as hydrogen peroxide, iodine or Betadine, Mercuroclear, rubbing alcohol)
- Baking soda
- Breakable (or instant) ice packs
- Cotton swabs
- Disposable syringe (w/o needle)
- Epipen (if children or adults have allergies)
- Fingernail clippers (your multi-purpose tool might have this, and if so you can dispense with it)
- Gauze bandage
- Gauze compress pads (2x2 individually wrapped pad)
- Hand sanitizer (use this in place of soap)
- Liquid antihistamine (not Benadryl tablets, however, as children should take liquid not pills; be aware that liquid antihistamines may cause drowsiness)
- Medical tape
- Moisturizer containing an anti-inflammatory
- Mole skin
- Pain reliever (aka aspirin; for children's pain relief, use liquid acetaminophen such Tylenol or liquid ibuprofen; never give aspirin to a child under 12)
- Poison ivy cream (for treatment)
- Poison ivy soap
- Powdered sports drinks mix or electrolyte additives
- Sling
- Snakebite kit
- Thermometer

- Tweezers (your multi-purpose tool may have this allowing you to dispense with it)
- Water purification tablets

If infants are with you, be sure to also carry teething ointment (such as Orajel) and diaper rash treatment.

Many of the items should be taken out of their store packaging to make placement in your fanny pack or backpack easier. In addition, small amounts of some items – such as baking soda and cotton swabs – can be placed inside resealable plastic bags, since you won't need the whole amount purchased.

Make sure the first-aid items are in a waterproof container. A re-sealable plastic zipper bag is perfectly fine. As Rocky Mountain National Park sports a moist climate, be sure to replace the adhesive bandages every couple of months, as they can deteriorate in the moistness. Also, check your first-aid kit every few trips and after any hike in which you've just used it, so that you can replace used components and to make sure medicines haven't expired.

If you have older elementary-age kids and teenagers who've been trained in first aid, giving them a kit to carry as well as yourself is a good idea. Should they find themselves lost or if you cannot get to them for a few moments, the kids might need to provide very basic first aid to one another.

Hiking with Children: Attitude Adjustment

To enjoy hiking with kids, you'll first have to adopt your child's perspective. Simply put, we must learn to hike on our kids' schedules – even though they may not know that's what we're doing.

Compared to adults, kids can't walk as far, they can't walk as fast, and they will grow bored more quickly. Every step we take requires three for them. In addition, early walkers, up to two years of age, prefer to wander than to "hike." Preschool kids will start to walk the trail, but at a rate of only about a mile per hour. With stops, that can turn a three-mile hike into a four-hour journey. Kids also won't be able to hike as steep of trails as you or handle as inclement of weather as you might.

This all may sound limiting, especially to long-time backpackers used to racking up miles or bagging peaks on their hikes, but it's really not. While you may have to put off some backcountry and mountain climbing trips for a while, it also opens to you a number of great short trails and nature hikes with spectacular sights that you may have otherwise skipped because they weren't challenging enough.

So sure, you'll have to make some compromises, but the payout is high. You're not personally on the hike to get a workout but to spend quality time with your children.

Family Dog

Dogs are part of the family, and if you have children, they'll want to share the hiking experience with their pets. In turn, dogs will have a blast on the trail, some larger dogs can be used as Sherpas, and others will defend against threatening animals.

But there is a downside to dogs. Many will chase animals and so run the risk of getting lost or injured. Also, a doggy bag will have to be carried for dog pooh – yeah, it's natural, but also inconsiderate to leave for other hikers to smell and for their kids to step in. In addition, most dogs almost always will lose a battle against a threatening animal, so there's a price to be paid for your safety.

Many places where you'll hike solve the dilemma for you as dogs aren't allowed on their trails. Dogs are verboten on some state and national parks trails but usually permitted on those in national forests. Always check with the park ranger before heading to the trail.

If you can bring a dog, make sure it is well behaved and friendly to others. You don't need your dog biting another hiker while unnecessarily defending the family.

Rules of the Trail

Ah, the woods or a wide open meadow, peaceful and quiet, not a single soul around for miles. Now you and your children can do whatever you want.

Not so fast.

Act like wild animals on a hike, and you'll destroy the very aspects of the wilds that make them so attractive. You're also likely to end up back in civilization, specifically an emergency room. And there are other people around. Just as you would wish them to treat you courteously, so you and your children should do the same for them.

Let's cover how to act civilized on the trail.

Minimize damage to your surroundings

When on the trail, follow the maxim of "Leave no trace." Obviously, you shouldn't toss litter on the ground, start rockslides, or pollute water supplies. How much is damage and how much is good-natured exploring is a gray area, of course. Most serious backpackers will say you should never pick up objects, break branches, throw rocks, pick flowers, and so on – the idea is not to disturb the environment at all.

Good luck getting a four-year-old to think like that. The good news is a four-year-old won't be able to throw around many rocks or break most branches.

Still, children from their first hike into the wilderness should be taught to respect nature and to not destroy their environment. While you might overlook a preschooler hurling rocks into a puddle, they can be taught to sniff rather than pick flowers. As they grow older, you can teach them the value of leaving the rock alone. Regardless of age, don't allow children to write on boulders or carve into trees.

Many hikers split over picking berries. To strictly abide by the "minimize damage" principle, you wouldn't pick any berries at all. Kids, however, are likely to find great pleasure in eating blackberries, currants and thimbleberries as ambling down the trail. Personally, I don't see any problem enjoying a few berries if the long-term payoff is a respect and love for nature. To minimize damage, teach them to only pick berries they can reach from the trail so they don't trample plants or deplete food supplies for animals. They also should only pick what they'll eat.

Collecting is another issue. In national and most state and county parks, taking rocks, flower blossoms and even pine cones is illegal. Picking flowers moves many species, especially if they are rare and native, one step closer to extinction. Archeological ruins are extremely fragile, and even touching them can damage a site.

But on many trails, especially gem trails, collecting is part of the adventure. Use common sense – if the point of the trail is to find materials to collect, such as a gem trail, take judiciously, meaning don't overcollect. Otherwise, leave it there.

Sometimes the trail crosses private land. If so, walking around fields, not through them, always is best or you could damage a farmer's crops.

Pack out what you pack in

Set the example as a parent: Don't litter yourself; whenever stopping, pick up whatever you've dropped; and always require kids to pick up after themselves when they litter. In the spirit of "Leave no trace," try to leave the trail cleaner than you found it, so if you come across litter that's safe to pick up, do so and bring it back to a trash bin in civilization. Given this, you may want to bring a plastic bag to carry out garbage.

Picking up litter doesn't just mean gum and candy wrappers but also some organic materials that take a long time to decompose and aren't likely to be part of the natural environment you're hiking. In particular, these include peanut shells, orange peelings, and eggshells.

Burying litter, by the way, isn't viable. Either animals or erosion soon will dig it up, leaving it scattered around the trail and woods.

Stay on the trail

Hiking off trail means potentially damaging fragile growth. Following this rule not only ensures you minimize damage but is also a matter of safety. Off trail is where kids most likely will encounter dangerous animals and poisonous plants. Not being able to see where they're stepping also increases the likelihood of falling and injuring themselves. Leaving the trail raises the chances of getting lost. Staying on the trail also means staying out of caves, mines or abandoned structures you may encounter. They are usually dangerous places.

Finally, never let children take a shortcut on a switchback trail. Besides putting them on steep ground upon which they could slip, their impatient act causes the switchback to erode.

Trail Dangers

On Rocky Mountain National Park trails, three common dangers face hikers – altitude sickness, lightning, and bad water. Fortunately, these threats are easily avoidable.

Altitude sickness

Since air pressure is lower at higher elevations, you will inhale less oxygen in mountainous areas. For most hikers, the problem begins when reaching 8,000 feet above sea level, in which acute mountain sickness can affect you.

More serious and deadlier problems can occur at higher than 12,000 feet, and parents shouldn't take their children above that level. Children will suffer from altitude sickness more readily than adults. As their bodies are still developing, they simply don't have the ability to adjust as quickly to changes in oxygen levels as do adults.

To avoid altitude sickness, go at a slow pace that allows time for your body to adjust to the changes. Limit altitude changes to no more than 2000-3000 feet so long as you're returning to your starting point.

Signs of altitude sickness include shortness of breath, dehydration, headache, nausea and dizziness. If you become confused, clumsy, vomit and have a dry cough, the condition is serious. Treating altitude sickness requires descending to a lower elevation where there's more oxygen. In addition, drink extra water to avoid dehydration, and eat light, high-carbohydrate meals. If the condition is serious, get medical attention immediately.

Lightning

Lightning provides a spectacular show for free, but it's also potentially quite deadly.

Once you hear thunder, lightning is not far off. Thunder is the traveling ripple caused by lightning's shock wave as it darts through the sky.

Rain need not be falling for lightning to hit you. An electrical storm is a major cause of lightning strikes.

To avoid lightning, you want to get away from places where it is most likely to strike: above the tree line on mountains; the mouth of a cave; a solitary tree; depressions; and ledges or wet ground.

When in the mountains, upon seeing lightning immediately descend to below the tree line. A thick tree grove is the best form of natural shelter. Remove metal from your body and sit on your backpack to keep you separated from the ground. Crouch as low as you can, shielding your head with your arms.

Bad water

When coming across a crystal clear stream or pond in the mountains, you may be tempted to drink from it or splash water on your face. Most backwoods streams are full of bacteria guaranteed to give you a bad tummy ache though. A major bacteria baddie in drinking water is Giardia lamblia, which sickens tens of thousands of people every year in the United States. Fortunately, it's not fatal if you're in good health and get immediate medical attention.

Only drink water you carry in. You also must avoid touching local water; if you get it on your hands or face, it can end up in your mouth, no matter how careful you are. If you must drink local water, there are three options: use water purification tablets, boil it, or use a reverse osmosis filter. The last two solutions probably aren't viable on a day hike.

Signs that you have imbibed bad water include stomach cramps, nausea, headaches, and diarrhea. Your body odor also may smell like sulfur. Drinking clean water is the remedy, but ultimately you need to get immediate medical attention.

For more about these topics and many others, pick up this author's "Hikes with Tykes: A Practical Guide to Day Hiking with Kids." You also can find tips online at the author's "Day

Hiking Trails" blog at *hikeswithtykes.blogspot.com*. Have fun on the trail!

Bonus Section II:
National Parks Primer

The breadth of wonders at America's national parks astounds the mind. You can stand at the nation's rooftop with 60 peaks taller than 12,000 feet at Rocky Mountain National Park or in a gash more than a mile deep in the earth at Grand Canyon. You can visit among the driest places in the world where little more than an inch of rain falls per year upon the beige sands of Death Valley or step into the ocean itself, such as Biscayne National Park where the bulk of the wilderness is the Atlantic and its vibrantly colored coral reefs. You can see some of the oldest rock on Earth, like the 1.2 billion year-old granite at Shenandoah National Park, to some of the newest land on the planet, as at Hawai'i Volcanoes National Park where you can watch lava flows create new ground inch by inch before you. You can enjoy parks that are primarily historical and even urban in nature, such as Cuyahoga Valley National Park, which features pioneer farms and bicycle paths, while others preserve breathless, awe-inspiring tracts of wilderness and stone, such as Yosemite's El Capitan and Half Dome. You can trek through caves with rooms larger than a foot-ball field situated hundreds of feet below the ground, such as at Carlsbad Caverns, or beneath trees soaring 15 stories over your head at Redwood National Park.

Given these grand wonders, not surprisingly national parks are a major travel destination. Indeed, many parks report record attendance during past few years. In 2017, annual attendance at parks operated by the National Parks Service hit 331 million visits – falling just short of its record number of visits set the previous year.

But with so many sights and given most national parks' distance from major population centers, how can visitors be sure they'll make the best use of their time and see all of the highlights?

Unfortunately, many park visitors treat a national park like a drive-in theater. Fully experiencing any nat-ional park requires that you "get out of the car," though. As W.H. Davies once wrote, "Now shall I walk/Or shall I ride?/'Ride,' Pleasure said; 'Walk,' Joy replied." A day hike can deliver the joy that each park offers.

What is (and isn't) a national park

Often local tourism agencies and business groups will refer to the "national park" near their community. If you've done any amount of traveling, such statements on websites and bro-chures would lead you to believe that there are hundreds of national parks!

The truth of that matter is that many of those agen-cies and hometown boosters actually are referring to units admin-istered by the National Park Service. The park service oversees more than 400 units, of which only 59 are actual national parks.

The types of units the park service manages are broken into more than 20 categories. Among the more common ones are national historical parks, national historic sites, national mon-uments, national memorials, national military parks, national battlefield parks, national battlefield sites, national battlefields, national preserves, and national reserves.

Other agencies also run parklands set aside for public use. The U.S. Forest Service overseas national forests. States and counties typically manage what are smaller versions of national parks and national forests. The U.S. Fish and Wildlife Service handles wildlife refuges while the Bureau of Land Management is in charge of wilderness areas.

As national forests and state parks adjoin national parks, travelers may not know when they've entered one unit or left another. Sometimes these different units even are operated as a single park, as is the case with the array of public lands protecting redwoods in north-western California, to save costs.

National parks generally are considered the crown jewels of the park service's outdoor experiences. When visiting a national park, though, don't discount the surrounding state parks, national forests, and other recreational areas, as they also offer excellent sights to see. They're also often less crowded than a national park.

Choosing a park to visit

Planning a trip to a national park isn't like going to the mall. Unless you're lucky enough to live near a nat-ional park, any trip to one will be part of a vacation for you and your family. So you'll need to choose which park you want to visit.

Your interests

Begin by asking what you'd most like to see. Do you want to watch wildlife? Experience great geological fea-tures like canyons and exotic rock formations? Of des-erts, volcanoes, autumn leaves, or tropical rain forests, which appeals to you? Are you interested in history? Was there a park you've always wanted to visit since childhood?

The quandary you'll face is that you'll want to see more than you probably have vacation time for!

Getting there

Next, decide how you'll reach the park. Many parks are remote and require driving, at least from a nearby airport. How much time you have to travel and how much money you're able to spend on transportation can help you narrow your list of potential parks to visit during a vacation.

Costs

After that, determine how much money is in your budget. The good news is that the park itself is fairly in-expensive to visit. As of press time, Congaree National Park in South Carolina and Cuyahoga Valley National Park in Ohio are absolutely free to enter while at the upper end Grand Canyon National Park charges $30 a vehicle for a week-long stay.

Sometimes fees are reduced (and even waived) for students and military personnel. Generally, the pass you purchase is good for a few days.

Many times a year, the park service offers "free entrance days." Expect the park to be crowded on those days, however, as they often coincide with holidays.

If you plan to hike national parks regularly, you should consider purchasing a National Parks and Federal Recreational Lands Pass, which will get a noncommercial vehicle plus passholder and three passengers into any national park for less than $100 a year.

Even less expensive versions of the pass are available for senior citizens, the disabled and National Park volunteers. If you visit a number of parks over several weeks, you'll definitely save on admission costs going this route.

Be forewarned that there may be additional fees if planning

to camp or to park an RV. Almost any hike that involves being part of a tour group at a major destination within a park carries a cost beyond the entry fee.

The real cost will come in lodging and food. Hotels within national parks generally are pricey while those near the park entrances only slight less so. Camping in the park or a neighboring national forest can be a good, inexpensive option. Food also can cost a small fortune within a park, but usually there are plenty of good, less expensive alternatives in nearby communities.

When to visit

Another consideration is when you will travel. Parts of some parks, such as Rocky Mountain, Crater Lake and Yosemite, actually cannot be reached during winter as heavy snowfall closes high mountain roads. Others, such as Death Valley, are simply too dangerous to hike in the summer heat. Most parks also have a peak season in which roads, campgrounds, sites and trails will be crowded; visiting a park when attendance is low, but the weather is ideal.

The high season typically is summer, running from Memorial Day through Labor Day weekends; those three-day weekends as well as when the Fourth of July falls on a Friday or Monday, usually draw the largest crowds in a year. In hot desert areas, the high season shifts slightly, as Death Valley and Arches national parks pull more people in late spring and early autumn when temperatures are pleasant.

The ideal time to visit is the off-season just before or just after high season. This can be difficult as usually high season coincides with when children are on school vacation.

Also think about the day of the week you will visit. You usually can avoid crowds by visiting weekdays, especially Monday through Thursday, when attendance dips. On three-day holiday weekends, sometimes the adjoining Thursday or Tuesday can see an uptick as well.

The time of day also plays a role. The earlier in the morning you can get to a national park, the less congested it will be on roadways and at popular sites. Usually, park visitors make their way from the nearest hotels mid-morning to the front gates and then set off again before sunset to their lodging. In addition, visitor centers at some parks will close for holidays, usually Christmas.

Of course, visiting during the off-season and on week-days comes with trade-offs. The weather may be cold or extremely hot; sometimes ranger-led park programs are nil on weekdays, especially in the off-season. In addition, access to some parks can be limited depending on the season. Yellowstone, for example, closes some of its entrances during winter as snowfall at the high elevations makes roads impassable. Other parks, such as Crater Lake, can't be reached at all during the off-season because of heavy snow.

Another possibility for avoiding crowds is to visit national parks that see low attendance overall. Yosemite, Yellowstone, the Grand Canyon and Cuyahoga national parks typically boast the highest attendance so definitely will be crowded during the high seasons. Great Basin (in Nevada) and Theodore Roosevelt (in North Dakota) national parks, however, are easy to reach but see few visitors compared to those in California, Arizona and Utah.

Pets

Pets are an important member of many families, and a vacation with them at a national park is possible, albeit with limitations.

Dogs and cats typically are only allowed in the park's developed areas, such as drive-in campgrounds and pic-nic areas, but rarely on trails. They also must be on a leash as well.

So if heading on a day hike, what to do with Rover or Queenie? Some parks offer kennels; short of that, one of your party will have to stay behind with the pet.

National forests surrounding the national park usu-ally have more lenient rules regarding pets, so if camp-ing you may want to consider pitching a tent there in-stead, though an adult member of the party still will have to stay with the dogs while everyone else hikes the national park.

Getting kids involved

Children obviously can benefit from visiting these great outdoors treasures. A trip to a national park will give any child fond memories that will literally last a lifetime. During their visit, they will experience their natural joy of discovery, certainly by seeing and exploring the sights themselves or perhaps through a touch table in which they get to feel fossils or a rabbit pelt at a visitor center. The visit alone will encourage their appreciation for nature. Take them on a hike through these wild areas, and they get the bonus of exercise in the fresh air.

The National Park Service offers a variety of great, interactive programs aimed at teaching kids about nature through fun and adventure. They often become the more memorable moments of a park visit for children, and a few even offer cool souvenirs at the end.

Among the programs:

• **Junior Ranger** – Most parks now offer some version of this program, in which kids by filling out a self-guided booklet and sometimes performing volunteer work can earn a Junior

Ranger patch or pin among other goodies.

• **Ranger-led activities** – Park rangers often host family-friendly activities on the park's geology, wildlife, ecology, history and other topics. Some parks during the evening offer programs in which kids can sit about a campfire and learn about nature.

• **Star parties** – Several national parks, especially those that are remote, offer nighttime viewings of the sky with telescopes. Your kids never will see a sky so brilliantly lit with stars.

• **Touch programs** – Some parks offer kids the opportunity to meet live animals or to touch cool found objects, such as turtle shells, feathers and rocks. They usually are held at the park's nature or visitor center.

Kids' activities aren't limited to just inside the park, however. Before even leaving on your trip, have your children:

• **Check out the park's website** – Many of the websites list activities specific to their park that later can be played on the drive to the park or during hikes.

• **Meet Smokey Bear virtually** – Younger kids can learn about forest fires and nature at Smokey Bear's official website: *www.smokeybear.com/kids*

• **Visit Webrangers** – Get kids excited about your trip with a stop at the Webrangers website (*www.nps.gov/webrangers*). Kids can play more than 50 online games that allow them to explore various national parks.

Hiking national parks tips

Day hiking usually isn't as simple as throwing on one's tennis shoes and hitting the trail. While that may be fine at a small city park, doing so in a national park can invite disaster. Though day hiking hardly requires as much gear or planning as a backpacking, you still need to bring some equipment and to think ahead.

Following these 10 simple guidelines should ensure your day hike is problem-free:

• **Know where you're going** – Look at a map of the trail before going out on it. Bring a paper map and com-pass with you on the trail and check both frequently as you walk.

• **Get the right footwear** – If your feet hurt, the hike is over. Good-fitting hiking boots almost always are a must on wilderness trails while cross-trainers probably are fine for paved surfaces; sandals almost always are a no-no.

• **Bring water** – You'll need about two pints of water per person for every hour of hiking and even more if in hot or dry climates. Leave soda and sugary fruit drinks at home; they are no replacement for water.

• **Layer your clothing** – Doing so allows you to remove and put back on clothing as needed to suit the weather. Make sure the layer next to the body wicks moisture away from the skin while the outer layer protects against wind and rain.

• **Carry a first-aid kit** – A small kit that allows you to bandage cuts and that contains some emergency equipment such as matches and a whistle will suffice for short hikes.

• **Don't overpack** – A lighter backpack always is better than one full of stuff you don't need. At the same time, don't skimp on the essentials so that you can safely complete the hike.

• **Use a trekking pole** – Unless the surface you're on is absolutely level, you'll find a walking stick helps reduce fatigue. This is especially true if you're carrying a backpack.

• **Follow the rules of the trail** – Leave no trace by not littering ("Pack out what you pack in.") and by staying on the trail. Don't deface rocks or destroy signage.

• **Don't forget a snack** – Trail mix as well as jerky can help you maintain energy on the trail. It's also a good motivator for any children with you.

• **Enjoy the journey** – Reaching the destination is never as important as having a good time on the way there. If with children, play games, pause when something grabs their attention, and never turn the hike into a death march.

Services and amenities

Services and amenities at national parks can vary greatly depending on the number of visitors and the part of the park you're in. You almost always can expect to find a visitor center and campgrounds with bathrooms; that doesn't mean there will be a restaurant or a vending machine with snacks and water on site, however.

If hoping to stay in a park lodge or at a campground, quickly make reservations; the same goes for hotels, motels and campgrounds near the park. A safe bet to ensure that a reservation can be made is make them at least six months ahead and up to a year in advance at the most popular parks.

Most parks have at least some trails available for those with disabilities to traverse. Be aware, however, that these trails may not head to a park's top sights.

Best sights to see

Which national park trails offer the best vistas? Lead to awesome waterfalls? Let you see wildlife? To enjoy fall colors? Here are some lists of the best national park trails for those and many other specific interests.

Beaches

Come summertime, there's almost no better place to be than the beach. The warmth of the sun upon your face, the sound of waves splashing against the shore, the blue water stretching into the horizon...Let's go!

Among the most beautiful beaches you can visit are those in national parks. Thousands of miles of shoreline around lakes and along oceans are protected in our parks, and just like the wildlife and rock formations you're apt to find in most of them the beaches won't disappoint either.

Here are six must-see beaches at our national parks.

Ocean Path Trail, Acadia National Park: Cobble beaches and hard bedrock make up most of the shoreline for the Atlantic Ocean that surrounds the Maine park's many islands. A rare exception is the 4.4-miles round trip Ocean Path Trail that heads from a sand beach to sea cliffs.

Convoy Point, Biscayne National Park: This boardwalk trail is flat and easy, running along the Florida mangrove shore known as Convoy Point. You'll follow the blue-green waters of Biscayne Bay and be able to spot some small, mangrove-covered islands. Bring a lunch; there's a picnic area below palms overlooking the bay. Part of the boardwalk also takes you out over the water. As the bay is shallow and quite clear, you'll have no trouble spotting the bottom.

Swiftcurrent Lake, Glacier National Park: The first 0.6 miles of the trail at this Montana park heads through an evergreen forest with several short spur trails leading to beaches along Swiftcurrent Lake. Meltwater from Grinnell Glacier feeds lake, making for an crystal clear albeit cold water.

Leigh Lake, Grand Teton National Park: Several alpine lakes perfect for a family outing sit at the Wyoming park's central String Lake Area. The 1.8-mile round trip trail heads around a shimmering blue lake through green pines with gray Mount Moran soaring in the background. During summer, enjoy a picnic on the beach and then a swim in the cool waters.

Ruby Beach Trail, Olympic National Park: The Washington park's Pacific Ocean shoreline features gushing sea stacks, piles of driftwood logs, and colorful, wave-polished stones. To enjoy all three, take the 1.4-mile Ruby Beach Trail. Some of the driftwood here has floated in from the distant Columbia River.

Coastal Trail, Redwood National Park: With more than 40 miles of pristine Pacific Ocean coastline, the northern California park is the perfect place to see tide pools and sea stacks. The latter are visible from many highway vistas but to get close up to a tide pool – a small body of saltwater that sustains many colorful sea creatures on the beach at low tide – explore the 1-mile segment (2-miles round trip) of the Coastal Trail at Enderts Beach south of Crescent City.

Fall colors

Ah, autumn – the world appears to have been repainted, as red, gold and sienna orange leaves contrast with the blue sky. For many travelers, fall is their favorite time to hit the road.

But there's more to see than the leaves. As those they fall to the ground, the landscape opens up, allowing you to spot interesting geological features or terrain that summer's green foliage keeps hidden. More animal sightings also are possible as birds migrate while mammals gorge in preparation for winter's cold. As the foliage no longer is as thick, seeing them is easier.

America's national parks offer a number of great places to experience autumn's beauty. And with summer vacation over, many of the parks will be less crowded.

Six national parks particularly deliver great autumn experiences for travelers.

Cuyahoga Falls National Park: Brandywine Falls ranks among the most popular of the Ohio park's several waterfalls. The area surrounding the falls is gorgeous in October beneath autumn leaves, and the Brandywine Gorge Trail to it is shaded

Cedar Creek and Abbey Island at Ruby Beach, Olympic National Park

almost the entire way by red maples and eastern hemlocks. With a combination of segments from the Stanford Road Metro Parks Bike and Hike Trail, the gorge trail loops 1.5 miles to the falls then back to the trailhead with several crossings of Brandywine Creek.

Great Sand Dunes National Park: Most people visit this Colorado park for the sand dunes soaring 60-plus stories in the sky. There's more to the park than dunes, though. The Montville Trail provides an excellent sample of that as it heads into the surrounding mountains. The 0.5-mile loop partially runs alongside a creek, where the golden canopy of cottonwood and aspen trees sends you to an autumn wonderland.

Great Smoky Mountains National Park: The 1-mile round trip Clingmans Dome Trail heads to the highest spot in the national park and Tennessee. Autumn leaves on the road to Clingmans Dome usually change about mid-October, offering a spectacular red, orange and yellow display. At the dome's top, views of those swaths of harvest colors can stretch for up to a hundred miles in all directions.

Hot Springs National Park: Though hardly thoughts of as a backcountry wilderness experience, the Arkansas park does offer a number of forested trails to enjoy. The best in autumn is the Hot Springs Mountain Trail. Heading through a beautiful mixed hardwood and pine forest, the route offers a gorgeous fall leaf display – and cooler temperatures than during muggy summer.

Shenandoah National Park: Spectacular autumn views await day hikers on the Stony Man Trail, a segment of the Appalachian National Scenic Trail. At the trail's top, you'll be rewarded with an expansive view of the Shenandoah Valley and the Massanutten and Allegheny Mountains beyond, their trees alit in harvest colors, as you breathe in clean, crisp air.

Death Valley National Park – OK, there are no autumn leaves here at all – but September's cooler temperatures ensure you actually can stand leave an air conditioned vehicle for a lot longer than a minute to experience the forbidding desert landscape. Among the best places in the California park to visit is the Golden Canyon Interpretive Trail, where you can learn to read rocks that tell the tale of how a lake once here vanished.

Romance

What are the most romantic places in the world? Paris? Hawaii? Italy?

Try a national park.

Though national parks often are thought of as places to get back to nature, they're also great spots to get a little closer to your sweetie. Among the romantic possibilities are moonbows, romantic vistas, desert oasis and incredible sunrises.

49 Palms Oasis, Joshua Tree National Park

Moonbow over waterfalls: At night during a full moon, moonbows often can be seen over waterfalls as the silvery light from the nearest heavenly body refracts off the mist. Plan a spring or early summer visit to Yosemite National Park when the moon is full. On a clear night, moonlit rainbows – called moonbows – span 2425-foot high Yosemite Fall with a trail leading right to its base.

Desert oasis: What is more romantic than midnight at the oasis? Joshua Tree National Park has a few, with the 49 Palms Oasis among the easiest to reach. The 49 Palms Oasis Trail heads 1.5-miles to stands of fan palms and water pools. Bring a blanket to lay out on the sand and a picnic basket for an evening snack under the stars.

Breathtaking vistas: For many, vistas of the Blue Ridge Mountains rank among the nation's most beautiful natural

Sunrise at Pu'u'ula'ula Summit, Haleakalā National Park

scenery. The 4-mile hike up to the summit of Old Rag Mountain via the Ridge Trail at Shenandoah National Park is challenging, but the 360 degree view from the top is unparalleled, as nearly 200,000 acres of wilderness stretch below you. Twirl your beloved around in a dance so that the entire scene spins before her eyes.

Stargazing: Boasting among the darkest skies in continental America, you can see up to 7,500 stars with the naked eye – nearly four times more than is typical in a rural area – at Bryce Canyon National Park. The Piracy Point Trail, a half-mile round trip from Far View Point, leads to a picnic area overlooking a cliff perfect for stargazing. Study up on the names of a few stars in the night sky and point them out to your sweetheart.

Fruitpicking: The Park Service at Capitol Reef National Park maintains more than 3,100 trees – including cherry, apricot, peach, pear and apple – in orchards planted decades ago by Mormon pioneers. For a small fee, park visitors can pick the fruit when in season. While there's no designated trail, the Historic Fruita Orchards Walk takes you through the fruit trees near Utah Hwy. 24. Share with your beloved what you've picked at your next rest stop.

Sunrise to propose by: At 10,023 feet, Pu'u'ula'ula Summit at Haleakalā National Park offers what many consider the world's most romantic sunrise. As the sun ascends over a blanket of clouds below the summit, it colors the crater from the inside out in an incredible light show. Bring a breakfast picnic and as the new day begins, propose marriage, for the sunrise symbolizes the dawning of your life together. Since you can drive to the summit, after she says "Yes," together hike one of the trails into the crater (either the Keonehe'ehe'e Trail or the Halemau'u Trail).

Sunrises and sunsets

Nothing quite so effectively displays Mother Nature's beauty than a sunrise or sunset, those few moments each day when the world shines golden and with incredible serenity.

Some of America's best sunrises and sunsets can be seen in her national parks. They range from the where the morning light first touches America each day to romantic sunsets over tropical waters, from the subtle signal for a million bats to begin their day to incredible sunrises over the continent's deepest chasm.

Here are seven must-see sunrises and sunsets at our national parks.

First sunrise at Acadia National Park: Day hikers can walk to one of the first spots where the sun touches America each morning via the South Ridge Trail in Maine's Acadia National

Park. The trail is a 7.2-miles round trip to the top of Cadillac Mountain, which is the highest summit on the Eastern seaboard. Though the hike would be done in the dark, with moonglow and flashlights, the trail is traversable. Acadia's ancient granite peaks are among the first places in the United States where the sunrise can be seen. Be sure to bring a blanket to lay out on the cold rock and take a seat looking southeast.

Gold-lined paths at Bryce Canyon: Fairyland really does exist – it's smack dab in southcentral in Utah, where a maze of totem pole-like rock formations called hoodoos grace Bryce Canyon National Park. Hoodoos are unusual landforms in which a hard caprock slows the erosion of the softer mineral beneath it. The result is a variety of fantastical shapes. Take the Queens Garden Trail, which descends into the fantasyland of hoodoos. When hiking during the early morning, sunrise's orange glow magically lights the trail's contours.

Bat show at Carlsbad Caverns: About 1 million Mexican Freetail bats live in Carlsbad Caverns. During the day, they rest on the ceiling of Bat Cave, a passageway closed to the public. At sunset, to feed for the evening, the bats dramatically swarm out of the cave in a tornadic-like spiral, their silhouettes stretching into the distant horizon. An open-air amphitheater allows visitors to safely watch the bats' departure in an event called The Night Flight. The Chihuahuan Desert Nature Trail, a half-mile loop, also allows you to watch the bats disperse across the New Mexican desert.

Breathtaking light show at Grand Canyon: Among the Grand Canyon National Park's most spectacular sights – sunrise and sunset – can be seen within walking distance of Grand Canyon Village in Arizona. While the South Rim Trail extends several miles along the canyon edge, you only have to walk to Mather Point, where views of the canyon shift like pictures in a

Hoodoo rock formations at Bryce Canyon ampitheater

marquee at both sunrise and sunset. Another great spot that's a little less crowded is Ooh Ahh Point on the South Kaibab Trail, which is east of the village and south of Yaki Point. The aptly named Ooh Ahh Point is less than 200 feet below the rim.

100-mile views at Great Smoky Mountains: You can enjoy views of sunrises and sunsets covering up to a hundred miles on the Clingmans Dome Trail in Great Smoky Mountains National Park. How incredible are the sunsets? They can be crowded, as those hoping to photograph the stunning scenery line up 45 minutes before the sun descends.

Romantic sunsets at Biscayne National Park: A full 95 percent of Florida's Biscayne National Park sits underwater, a turquoise blue paradise laced with vividly colored coral reefs – and nothing quite says romance like a sunset over this tropical ocean. Adams Key offers a quarter-mile trail from the dock through the hardwood hammock on the island's west side; most of the route skirts the beach, where the sunset can be enjoyed.

Needles aglow at Canyonlands National Park: Clambering over boulders and ambling across strangely angled slickrock – and watching needles aglow at sunset – await on Canyonlands National Park's Slickrock Trail in southeastern Utah. The 2.9-mile loop trail generally follows a mesa rim. Plan to walk the trail about an hour or so before sunset; on the final mile, tall thin rock formations called needles fill the horizon, glowing crimson as the sun sets.

Vistas

Certainly the best memories of any trip are the great vistas enjoyed along the way. For some, the beauty of the natural scene before them ranks far above any man-made art. For others, the diminutiveness experienced upon seeing an incredible panorama is a spiritual moment.

America's national parks fortunately preserve the most impressive of these vistas. But other than a sign right at the entry road, how does one know where they are? No worries – we've compiled a list of the six best vistas at our national parks, all of which are easy to reach with short hikes.

Great Smoky Mountains National Park, Clingmans Dome: You can enjoy views of up to a hundred miles atop one of the highest points east of the Mississippi River. The 1-mile round trip Clingmans Dome Trail heads to the highest spot in Great Smoky Mountains National Park and Tennessee and the third tallest east of the Mississippi. The top rewards with an incredible 360 degree panorama. A verdant spruce-fir forest sits at the ridge tops while in autumn the leaves of hardwoods below adds swaths of harvest colors. On clear days, 100-mile views are possible.

Grand Canyon National Park, South Rim: Perhaps the

South Rim, Grand Canyon National Park

most fantastic vista in all of North America is the Grand Canyon's South Rim. Indeed, the Grand Canyon rightly defies description. Most who see it for the first time say it reminds them of a majestic painting, appropriately suggesting it's a place that only can be visualized by actually gazing at it. While the South Rim Trail extends several miles along the canyon edge, a short section east of the El Tovar Hotel offers the best views. You'll be able to see the Colorado River a mile below and an array of incredible buttes, towers and ridges and that stretch up to 10 miles away on the canyon's other side.

Yosemite National Park, Yosemite Valley: Two sweeping views of Yosemite Valley await on the Sentinel Dome and Taft Point Loop. Located south of the valley along Glacier Point Road, the trail runs 4.9-miles. Taft Point allows you to get right up to the edge of the valley rim, offering magnificent views of

Yosemite Valley below and Yosemite Fall (the tallest in North America) and El Capitan across the way. The 360 degree views from the top of Sentinel Dome – which peaks at 8127 feet – are the hike's highlight. Among the visible sights are Yosemite Valley, Half Dome, El Capitan, Yosemite Falls, North Dome, and Basket Dome.

Yellowstone National Park, Fairy Falls Trail: The multi-col-ored Grand Prismatic Spring and an array of geysers can be seen on the first 0.6 miles of Yellowstone's Fairy Falls Trail. A 400-foot stretch of the trail appropriately known as Picture Hill provides a grand vista of the spring. About 370 feet in diameter, Grand Prismatic is the largest hot spring in the United States and the third largest in the world. It reaches a depth of 121 feet. Be sure to bring polarized sunglasses. By wearing them, you can see the spring's rainbow colors reflected in the steam rising off the water. The smaller Excelsior Geyser Crater sits beyond the geological wonder.

Zion National Park, Canyon Overlook Trail: You can hike past hoodoos to a vista that affords a fantastic view of Zion National Park's famous Beehives, East Temple, the Streaked Wall, and the Towers of the Virgin, on the Canyon Overlook Trail. The 1-mile round trip of pinnacles, arches and domes feels like a walk on an alien world straight out of a science fiction film. Summer temps are cooler in the morning and late evening.

Mesa Verde National Park, Park Point: Park Point, Mesa Verde's highest spot at 8572 feet above sea level with 360 degree views, is often touted as the most impressive vista in the United States. The 0.5-mile round trip Park Point Overlook Trail takes you to the view of Montezuma and Mancos valleys, and on a clear day, you can see four states – Colorado, Utah, Arizona and New Mexico. Add 0.5-miles round trip to the fire lookout tower for additional great views.

Yosemite Falls, Yosemite National Park

Waterfalls

Nothing quite demonstrates the awesome power and beauty of Mother Nature like a waterfall – hundreds of gallons of water rushing several stories over a cliffside, the vertical stream nestled in lush greenery, the mist and droplets that splash on you at the fall's base.

Fortunately, several of our national parks preserve many of the country's most fantastic falls. Many of them are quire easy to reach via short hikes.

Yosemite Falls: If there is one waterfall that everyone absolutely must see, it's this one in California's Yosemite National Park. Actually consisting of seven waterfalls, Yosemite Falls sends water rushing 2,425 feet downward into the valley. Depending on snow melt, the falls' peak flow typically occurs in May when up to 2,400 gallons of water flow down Yosemite Falls every second.

You can hike 1.2-miles round trip to the base of North America's tallest waterfall. During spring, you may want to take the trail on a clear night when the moon is full, especially if on a romantic trip. Moonlit rainbows – called moonbows – span the waterfalls.

Queenie and Fido also can enjoy the waterfalls, as leashed dogs are allowed on the trail. Be sure that your dog is comfortable with crowds and other people, however.

Tokopah Falls: Not many travelers have heard of Tokopah Falls, but it's an incredible site. A series of cascades, it drops 1200 feet – almost the height of the Empire State Building – at California's Sequoia National Park. It's a park of tall trees and tall waterfalls. A glacier carved Tokopah Valley, leaving high gray cliff walls that cradle a meadow, creeks, and a pine and fir forest. The 3.8-mile (600 foot elevation gain) Tokopah Falls Trail leads to its namesake, which is the park's highest waterfall.

Avalanche Lake waterfalls: With melting glaciers and high mountains, waterfalls can be found aplenty in Montana's Glacier National Park. Melting glaciers feed several lakes across the park, including Avalanche Lake. Start on the Trail of the Cedars then turn off onto the Avalanche Lake Trail. The 4.7-miles round trip (505-foot gain) trail heads to Avalanche Lake, where several waterfalls from Sperry Glacier drop several hundred feet to fill the valley with its turquoise waters.

Hidden Falls: You can enjoy this waterfall and then a vista at 7200 feet elevation on Grand Teton National Parks' Hidden Falls-Inspiration Point Trail. The trail runs 3.8-miles round trip into Cascade Canyon. Though technically not a waterfall but a series of cascades running 200 feet over several multiple steps, Wyoming's Hidden Falls still impresses. Because only part of the cascades are steep, there's a lot of confusion among various sources about exactly how high the drop that looks most like

Hidden Falls, Grand Teton National Park

a waterfall actually is – some say 80 feet and others say 100. Afterward, visit Inspiration Point, a short walk from the falls.

Fairy Falls: The trail to Fairy Falls at Yellowstone National Park offers a three-for-one deal: the multi-colored Grand Prismatic Spring, an array of geysers, and the 197-foot waterfall. If going to see Old Faithful, this is a perfect nearby trail to hike the same day. The 5.6-mile hike begins with geysers then arrives Grand Prismatic Spring, a wonder that boasts multicolored rings of algae. Fairy Falls comes next. The waterfalls' base supports a variety of vegetation. If looking for a place to picnic, the rocks downstream from the falls where raspberry bushes grow make a perfect spot.

Marymere Falls: A trail through a lush, old growth forest that ends at this waterfall will delight anyone hiking the Marymere Falls Trail at Olympic National Park in Washington. The 1.6-mile round trip trail really is like taking two entirely different hikes in one. Most of the trail heads through a intensely green Pacific Northwest rain forest while the last portion at the destination is purely about the waterfalls. Marymere Falls is about 90 feet high, and you'll get really close to it as the trail passes the small plunge pool. Hikers also can take a stairs to see the falls' upper segment. A few landings on the stairs offers fantastic views of the falls from different angles.

Laurel Falls: Though Rainbow Falls is the tallest at Great Smoky Mountains National Park, many visitors eschew it because of the strenuous hike. One that's much easier to reach and still spectacular in its own right is Tennessee's 80-foot Laurel Falls. The Laurel Falls Trail runs 2.6-miles round trip through a pine-oak woods with hemlock and beech along the stream, making for a colorful walk in autumn. May also is impressive, as mountain laurel blooms along the trail and near the falls, which runs its highest that month. Deer, often with fawns, wood squirrels, and songbirds are common on the trail. The waterfall on Laurel Branch consists of an upper and a lower section. A wide walkway crosses the stream where the mist from the falls roils over her head.

Brandywine Falls: This 65-foot waterfalls awaits visitors on the Brandywine Gorge Trail at Ohio's Cuyahoga Valley National Park. The Brandywine Gorge Trail loops 1.5 miles to the falls then back to the trailhead with several crossings of Brandywine Creek. The area surrounding the falls is gorgeous in October beneath autumn leaves, but the trail can be hiked any season. It's shaded almost the entire way by red maples with eastern hemlocks and green moss upon the ground once closer to the falls.

Wildflowers
From rare California poppies to sweet-scented phlox, wild-

Catawba rhododendron blooms, Great Smoky Mountains National Park

flowers begin to bloom this month across much of the country. Filling green meadows, desert basins, and forest floors, wildflowers bring a special beauty that usually can only be seen for a few weeks.

Our national parks rank among the best places to enjoy wildflowers. As those parks cover wide swaths of protected land, they offer ample area for massive blooms, enhancing the already beautiful scenery.

Here are six not-to-miss spots at our national parks for spotting wildflowers from now through summer.

Pinnacles National Park: Each spring, brilliant orange California poppies, lavender-colored bush lupine, and white mariposa lilies blossom across the nation's newest national park. To see a variety of them at different elevations and from a number of vistas, take the High Peaks and Bear Gulch trails.

Great Smoky Mountains National Park: About the same time on the other side of the continent, the forest floor on the Mingus Creek Trail turns fragrant with the pleasant sent of blue phlox. Several other shade-loving flowers also can be found along the creek, including violets, Virginia bluebells and white trillium. During late April, expect to see flame azalea in bloom on the Deep Creek/Indian Falls trails. In May, look for mountain laurel, and in June for rhododendron.

Glacier National Park: From late June through early August, summer wildflower blooms are at their peak. Check out the Swiftcurrent Lake Loop Trail for meadows strewn with purple asters, white torch-shaped clusters of beargrass, and sun yellow glacier lilies, all with majestic mountains as a backdrop.

Sequoia National Park: Next to the world's largest trees are blossoms that somehow manage to stand out despite their size. On the Crescent Meadow Trail in early July, lavender Mustang clover with yellow centers look like little pins of brilliant light against the immense pine cones that have fallen into the grass.

Crater Lake National Park: Wildflowers usually bloom along the stream next to the Annie Creek Trail and across the meadows from mid-July through August. Among those that might be spotted are Macloskey's violet, big huckleberry, sulphur flower, Crater Lake currant, western mountain ash, and wax currant.

Great Basin National Park: Amid the high desert is an oasis of summer wildflowers on the Alpine Lakes Trail. Spring-fed Lehman Creek flows into a lake and supports Parry's primrose, penstemon, and phlox, all set against vibrant green grass. Butterflies are abundant here as well.

Wildlife

America's national parks are known for their great vistas and fantastic rock formations, but they also preserve another treasure: wildlife.

Bison at Lamar Valley, Yellowstone National Park

In fact, national parks rank among the best places to see interesting and rare wildlife. Late summer marks a particularly good time for wildlife viewing at many parks as most mothers bring out their young by that time of the year.

Given the breadth of national park locations, there's also the opportunity to see almost every kind of North American wildlife, from those that live on mountains, in marine environments, and in the tropics to those that make their homes on prairies, deserts, and in temperate forests.

Mountains: Travelers can explore the "Serengeti of North America" on the Lamar Valley Trail at Wyoming's Yellowstone National Park. Like the mountain-ringed African plain, Lamar Valley serves as home to the classic megafauna that define North America. Bison, elk, grizzlies, black bears, wolves, coyotes, eagles, osprey and more all can be found at this high elevation. Coyotes also can be seen wandering about, looking for a meal while bald eagles and osprey grace the skies. Grizzlies reside in the hilly woods, but they and the area's other big two predators – black bears and wolf packs – prefer to remain under cover than be seen.

Marine: You can encounter an array of marine wildlife on the Beach Trail at Alaska's Glacier Bay National Park. Low tide also provides an opportunity to see intertidal life. As the waters retreat into the ocean – and water levels here can fall 25 vertical feet, among the greatest extremes in the world – a number of animals and plants are exposed. Don't be surprised to spot starfish and snails on the sands and grasses. On shore, a variety of sea birds gather and fly over, often nabbing exposed intertidal creatures for a meal. During those first moments of sunlight, watch for humpback whales, harbor porpoise, puffins, sea otters, and Steller sea lions, frolicking and feeding in the mouth of the bay. Bring binoculars. If lucky, you'll also hear the blow of humpback whales.

Tropics: Tropical wildlife can be safely seen from the Anhinga Trail at Florida's Everglades National Park. The trail's boardwalk takes you over open water where you can watch for alligators peeking out of a river, as well as turtles, herons and egrets. Winter marks the best season to see the most wildlife. A number of birds spend their time in the Everglades after migrating from a northern clime. Among those you can spot are the double breasted cormorant, great egret, great blue heron, snowy egret, tricolored heron, white ibis and woodstork. Turkey vultures congregate in the marsh during the early morning hours.

Prairies: North America's largest mammal – the bison – freely roams North Dakota's Theodore Roosevelt National Park, and the Buckhorn Trail is an excellent place to spot them and other Great Plains wildlife. The trail includes a prairie dog

Gila woodpecker, Saguaro National Park

town that stretches for about a mile. You'll be able to spot them barking from their burrow entrances as they keep an eye out for predators. Hawks, coyotes and rattlesnakes are among the creatures hoping to make an unsuspecting prairie dog its dinner.

Deserts: Four desert ecosystems can be found in North America, and the park closest to a major metro area offers among the best spots to see wildlife of these dry climes. Outside of Tucson, Ariz., Saguaro National Park's Douglas Spring Trail crosses the Rincon Mountain District (Saguaro Park East), providing the chance to see coyotes, roadrunners, jackrabbits, quail and Gila woodpeckers. All five of those creatures thrive in the Sonoran Desert, which stretches across Arizona and northern Mexico, as well as good portions of the continent's other three desert ecosystems.

Temperate forests: Great Smoky Mountains National Park, though stretching across the Appalachian Mountains, offers the opportunity to see many of the animals that reside in temperate forests covering much of the continent east of the Mississippi River. The Deep Creek/Indian Falls trails in the park's North Carolina section sports Eastern cottontail rabbit, groundhogs, river otter, and white-tailed deer. Also present but much more elusive, as they keep to themselves, are black bear, bobcat, coyote, red fox, red wolf, and wild boar.

Winter

Most travelers think of summer as the best time to hit national parks – but winter also offers several spectacular sights that make for memorable visits.

So when the snow starts falling, consider a road trip to one of the following parks.

Birders paradise: Winter marks the best time to hike Florida's Everglades National Park, as the subtropical climate means unbearably hot and buggy summers. Indeed, a number of birds already know this and spend their time in the Everglades after migrating from a northern clime. Among those you can spot on the Anhinga Trail are the double breasted cor-

Golden Canyon, Death Valley National Park

morant, great egret, great blue heron, snowy egret, tricolored heron, white ibis and woodstork; turkey vultures congregate during the early morning hours.

Wildlife sightings: Leafless trees and snow's white backdrop makes sighting large wildlife a lot easier in winter than summer. The Warner Point Nature Trail on the south rim of Colorado's Black Canyon of the Gunnison National Park offers the chance to spot elk and Rocky Mountain bighorn sheep. Look for the elk in clearings and the bighorn sheep on the rocky cliff sides.

Heavy waterfalls: At most parks, waterfalls are most active in spring and early summer, thanks to snow melts. Not so at Washington state's Olympic National Park. Rain is more likely there during winter, meaning the water flow is higher, making for a more spectacular creeks and falls. One good trail through the park's lush, old growth forest that ends at a waterfall is the Marymere Falls Trail.

Bearable heat: During summer, unbearable heats makes California's Death Valley National Park at best a pass through seen from a motor vehicle. The park's average high in January is a pleasant 67 degrees, though, making winter the perfect time to walk the foreboding desert landscape. Among those sights is the lowest point in North America. Badwater Basin sits 282 feet below sea level and can be accessed in a mile-long round trip hike.

Avoid the crowds: Visitation drops during winter at most parks, so the trade-off for bundling up in coat, cap and gloves is seeing the great scenery without all of the crowds. A good bet is Yosemite National Park's spectacular Yosemite Valley in California. The Lower Yosemite Fall Trail offers a number of fantastic views of Yosemite Falls in a 1.2-mile loop with the added coolness of falling water frozen in mid-flight on the granite rocks.

Christmas

A little secret: Among the best ways to escape holiday stress is a national park trip. Though often thought of as a summer destination, only a couple of the parks close in winter, and almost all offer warm, cozy and peaceful holiday experiences. A bonus is that almost all parks are less crowded during winter.

Here are five great holiday-themed must-do's at our national parks.

Winter wonderland, Yellowstone National Park: Book a getaway at the Old Faithful Snow Lodge, which can only be reached this time of year by snow coach or snowmobile. The Christmas-decorated lodge keeps its fireplace burning with plenty of hot cocoa for visitors. During the day, hike past "ghost

Christmas caroling in the cavern, Mammoth Cave National Park

trees," formed when the steam from the Old Faithful geyser freezes on pine tree needles. Bison with snow-covered manes often feed across the geyser valley.

Polar Express train ride, Cuyahoga Valley National Park: Each December prior to Christmas, the Cuyahoga Valley Scenic Railroad's Polar Express chugs through the scenic Ohio park. Among the highlights on the refurbished passenger train is a reading of the children's book "Polar Express," which inspired a movie and this trip. Many passengers ride the train in their pajamas! If in the Southwest, a private company also runs a Polar Express to Grand Canyon National Park.

Luminaria-lit skiing: Denali National Park: Every December, rangers light the small paper lanterns that line ski trails at the Alaska park. Visitors also can snowshoe or stroll the route, which leaves from the Murie Science and Learning

Center, Denali's Winter Visitor Center. Several other National Park Service sites offering luminaria displays and hikes including Florida's De Soto National Memorial and Arizona's Tonto National Monument.

Snowshoe wildlife hike, Rocky Mountain National Park: Ranger-led snowshoe tours lead visitors of this Colorado park to a variety of wildlife, including elk, coyotes, deer and snowshoe hares. The trail is utterly quiet as snow-capped mountains and evergreens rise around you on all sides.

Caroling in a cave, Mammoth Cave National Park: In early December, the Kentucky park holds Christmas carol singing in the world's longest cave system. It's a tradition that goes back to 1883 when local residents held the first Christmas celebration in the cave's passageways.

Historical sites

While the National Park Service's 59 major parks largely focus on protecting natural wonders and wilderness, they also preserve some historical sites. While many are merely ruins, others are in just as good of shape (if not better) than when they originally stood.

Historic Fort Jefferson: At Dry Tortugas National Park, you can visit a fort used during the Civil War. Built with more than 16 million bricks during the mid-1800s, Fort Jefferson is the Western Hemisphere's largest masonry structure. Six walls and towers with a moat make up the fort's outer area on Garden Key.

19th Century Mining Town: Crossing a thick rolling woodland, the Colorado River Trail at Rocky Mountain National Park offers nice views of Colorado River, arguably the Southwest's most important waterway. The trail to the ruins of an 19th century mining town, Lulu City, in a 6.2-miles round trip with 320-

John Oliver cabin in Cades Cove, Great Smoky Mountains National Park

foot elevation gain.

Appalachian life: A number of great day hikes allow visitors to explore the Great Smoky Mountain National Park's rich history. Pioneer cabins and mills await on several short day hikes, including those at Cades Code and Mingus Mill.

Butterfield Stage station: Along the Texas-New Mexico border, families can step back into the Old West and experience the remoteness of what once was a welcome sign to travelers: a Butterfield Stage station in the Guadalupe Mountains. The 0.75-mile round trip Pinery Trail marks a great day hike for families at Guadalupe National Park. The trail leads to the ruins of the Pinery Station, a once favored stop on the original 2,800-mile Butterfield Overland Mail Route.

Trees

Among the most fantastical sights at our national parks are

trees. Whether they be gigantic, fossilized, or older than the hills (figuratively speaking), they're certain to awe. Here are six great tree sites to visit.

Sequoias: Your family will feel like hobbits walking through scenes from "The Lord of the Rings" movies on the General Grant Tree Trail at Kings Canyon National Park. The 0.5-mile trail heads through the General Grant Grove of giant sequoias. More than 120 sequoias in the grove exceed 10 feet in diameter and most tower several stories over your head.

Redwoods: Hiking families can enjoy a trip into what feels like the forest primeval on a segment of the Damnation Creek Trail in Redwood National Park. For those with younger children, a 1.2-mile round trip through just the redwoods section of the trail makes for more than an incredible, inspiring walk.

Bristlecone pines: On several of Great Basin National Park's glacial moraines rise incredibly ancient bristlecone pines, many nearly 5,000 years old, meaning they began growing as the ancient Egyptians built the pyramids. The 2.8-mile round trip Bristlecone Pine Trail allows you to walk among a grove of the trees, which scientists say likely are the oldest living organisms on Earth.

Joshua trees: Day hikers can enjoy a walk through a large Joshua tree forest in the desert above the Palm Springs, Calif., area. A segment of the Boy Scout Trail at Joshua Tree National Park runs through a grove for a 2.4-mile round trip. Technically not a tree, the unusual Joshua tree is a member of the lily family.

Chestnut trees: Day hikers can head through what used to be a grove of majestic chestnut trees. The Cades Cove Nature Trail runs 1.4-miles round trip trail (from the parking lot) and sits in Cades Cove, an isolated mountain valley that is a popular destination thanks to many well-preserved structures from

Base of General Grant Tree, Kings Canyon National Park

pioneer days. A few seedlings of the great chestnut remain.

Petrified forest: Families can hike the remains of a woodlands dating from the dinosaurs' earliest days on the Great Logs Trail in Petrified Forest National Park. The fairly easy walk consists of two loops that combine for a 0.6-mile round trip. Because of the hot Arizona weather, spring and autumn mark the best time to hike the trail.

Learn more about these and many other great national park trails in the author's "Best Sights to See at America's National Parks."

About the Author

Rob Bignell is a long-time hiker, editor, and author of the popular "Best Sights to See," "Hikes with Tykes," "Headin' to the Cabin," and "Hittin' the Trail" guidebooks and several other titles. He and his son Kieran have been hiking together for the past decade. Rob has served as an infantryman in the Army National Guard and taught middle school students in New Mexico and Wisconsin. His newspaper work has won several national and state journalism awards, from editorial writing to sports reporting. In 2001, *The Prescott Journal*, which he served as managing editor of, was named Wisconsin's Weekly Newspaper of the Year. Rob and Kieran live in Wisconsin.

CHECK OUT THESE OTHER HIKING BOOKS BY ROB BIGNELL

"Best Sights to See" series:
• America's National Parks
• Great Smoky Mountain National Park
• Voyageurs National Park

"Hikes with Tykes" series:
• Hikes with Tykes: A Practical Guide to Day Hiking with Children
• Hikes with Tykes: Games and Activities

"Headin' to the Cabin" series:
• Day Hiking Trails of Northeast Minnesota
• Day Hiking Trails of Northwest Wisconsin

"Hittin' the Trail" series:
National parks
• Grand Canyon National Park (ebook only)
Minnesota
• Gooseberry Falls State Park
• Split Rock Lighthouse State Park
Minnesota/Wisconsin
• Interstate State Park
• St. Croix National Scenic Riverway
Wisconsin
• Barron County
• Bayfield County
• Burnett County (ebook only)

- Chippewa Valley (Eau Claire, Chippewa, Dunn, Pepin counties)
- Crex Meadows Wildlife Area (ebook only)
- Douglas County
- Polk County
- St. Croix County
- Sawyer County
- Washburn County

GET CONNECTED!

Follow the author to learn about other great trails and for useful hiking tips:
- Blog: *hikeswithtykes.blogspot.com*
- Facebook: *dld.bz/fBq2C*
- Google+: *dld.bz/fBq2s*
- LinkedIn: *linkedin.com/in/robbignell*
- Pinterest: *pinterest.com/rbignell41*
- Twitter: *twitter.com/dayhikingtrails*
- Website: *dayhikingtrails.wordpress.com*

If you enjoyed this book,
please take a few moments to write a review of it.

Thank you!

www.ingramcontent.com/pod-product-compliance
Lightning Source LLC
Chambersburg PA
CBHW050355280326
41933CB00010BA/1477